Boost Your MCAT Score with Quick Techniques

Cindy .P Vu

Funny helpful tips:

Stay informed about the potential of liquid biopsies; they promise non-invasive disease detection.

Seek feedback from customers; it provides insights for improvement.

Boost Your MCAT Score with Quick Techniques : Maximize Your MCAT Success with Proven Test-Taking Strategies and Tips

Life advices:

Stay committed; dedication is key to overcoming challenges.

Your essence is a light; let it shine brightly, illuminating the way for others.

Introduction

This is a comprehensive resource designed to provide aspiring medical students with essential information about the Medical College Admission Test (MCAT). This guide covers various aspects of the MCAT, from its importance to registration, preparation strategies, test day tips, and its impact on medical school admissions.

The guide starts by introducing what the MCAT is and its significance in the medical school application process. It explains the structure of the MCAT, its scoring, and what constitutes a good MCAT score. Readers are then guided through the registration process, including eligibility, timing, fees, and options for rescheduling or canceling the test. Information on financial aid and accommodations is also provided.

The guide addresses the optimal timing for taking the MCAT, discussing when the test is offered and what classes are necessary to prepare effectively. It emphasizes the importance of knowing when one is ready to take the exam, cautioning against taking it too soon. Special advice is offered to nontraditional students.

The heart of the guide focuses on how to study for the MCAT. It provides various resources, such as podcasts, books, diagnostic tests, and prep courses, to aid in preparation. The guide explores the benefits of study groups and private tutors, while also discussing common pitfalls in the preparation process and how to manage stress.

Retaking the MCAT is also covered, including factors to consider when deciding to retake the test and how to prepare effectively for a retake. Readers are informed about the concept of voiding the exam and how it can be used as a practice tool.

Last-minute tips, test day logistics, and strategies to increase one's score are provided. The guide delves into the effects of the MCAT on medical school admissions, including what constitutes a competitive score, retaking considerations, timing, and its role in balancing a low GPA.

The guide concludes with a call to action, encouraging readers to prepare for the MCAT and providing resources for further study.

With a detailed breakdown of test sections, question types, strategies, and practice materials, this book serves as a valuable companion for anyone aspiring to succeed in the challenging world of medical school admissions.

Contents

CHAPTER 1
WHAT IS THE MCAT?

The Medical College Admissions Test, also known as the MCAT, is the standardized test administered by the Association of American Medical Colleges (AAMC) that students need to take for admission into US and Canadian medical schools. It is a computer based standardized test to help gauge the aspiring physician's ability to solve problems, think critically, and understand their knowledge of natural, behavioral, and social sciences. Medical school admissions committees use this information as part of their admissions process to determine if you will be a good fit for their school.

If you are a premed student and haven't heard of the MCAT, don't worry; many students don't know about it until it's nearly time to take it.

The MCAT will be one of the biggest hurdles you'll need to overcome on your journey to becoming a physician. It is a full day experience with over six hours of testing, plus another hour and a half consisting of breaks and other parts of the process. We like to call the MCAT a standardized test on steroids. It's no wonder so many premed students are terrified of taking the MCAT—it requires years of prerequisites and months of preparation.

Further into the book, we'll discuss how to best prepare for the MCAT. One of the most important things you should know as you begin to prepare for it, though, is that the MCAT is not necessarily a test used to assess your total knowledge base. Instead, it helps if you see it as a test to gauge how well you can analyze and critically think through the questions in front of you. Too many students take the same approach to the MCAT as they do the rest of the exams in their life, and they end up getting a less-than-great score. We'll show you how to avoid this mistake later on.

Ultimately, your MCAT score (or scores) is only one component of your medical school application and will be considered alongside a number of other factors to determine whether you gain entry into a particular program or not.

Why is the MCAT important?

The MCAT provides medical school admission committees with a standardized form of assessment for processing the thousands of applications that are submitted to their school each year. Unlike GPA (which differs depending on the school, the professor, and possibly the class), the MCAT is scored according to a universal rubric that allows for comparison of students from any institution.

Initially developed in 1928 to deal with the large dropout rate among first-year medical students, the MCAT was established with the intention of helping schools filter out students with little potential to succeed in their programs.[1]

In medical school admissions today, however, a number of factors influence the committee's decision to accept or reject a particular student. In addition to the MCAT score, grades, letters of reference, personal statements, extracurriculars, and other facets of a student's background are taken into consideration when assessing the application. Ultimately, admission committees aim to choose candidates who they believe will thrive in their specific medical school for that specific year.

Nontraditional Students

If you're a nontraditional student (someone who has taken some time off from college or maybe changed careers), you are a little unique when it comes to studying for the MCAT. Because many nontraditional students apply to medical school after taking a few (or more) years off in between completing their undergraduate study, the MCAT enables programs to judge how well they can still handle difficult standardized tests—something that will become a regular thing during medical school.

What is the structure of the MCAT?

The MCAT is a constantly evolving exam, regularly restructured to be compatible with the changing nature of medicine. The most current format, implemented in 2015, was developed by the AAMC after exhaustive interviews and surveys with medical school faculty and admissions committees.

Questions can either be passage-based or discrete. Discrete questions are one-off questions that don't require any other information to answer. Passage-based questions require you to read up to several paragraphs of information to help you answer the questions presented. Each passage will have several questions associated with it.

The MCAT currently consists of four sections, breaks, and other aspects of the test, in this specific order:

Tutorial (Optional)
10 minutes

Chemical and Physical Foundations of Biological Systems (Chem/Phys)
A 95-minute section consisting of 59 multiple-choice questions, testing basic biochemistry, biology, general (inorganic) chemistry,

organic chemistry, and physics.

Break (Optional)
10 minutes

Critical Analysis and Reasoning Skills (CARS)
A 90-minute section consisting of 53 multiple-choice questions, testing reading comprehension.

Lunch Break (Optional)
30 minutes

Biological and Biochemical Foundations of Living Systems (Bio/Biochem)
A 95-minute section consisting of 59 multiple-choice questions, testing basic biology, organic chemistry, inorganic chemistry, and biochemistry.

Break (Optional)
10 minutes

Psychological, Social and Biological Foundations of Behavior (Psych/Soc)
A 95-minute section consisting of 59 multiple-choice questions, testing introductory psychology, sociology, and biology.

Question about Voiding
5 minutes to determine if you want to void the test

Satisfaction Survey (Optional)
5 minutes

MCAT Overview		
Chemical and Physical Foundations of Biological Systems (Chem/Phys)	95 minutes	
	59 questions	
Critical Analysis and Reasoning Skills (CARS)	90 minutes	
	53 questions	
Biological and Biochemical Foundations of Living Systems (Bio/Biochem)	95 minutes	
	59 questions	
Psychological, Social, and Biological Foundations of Behavior (Psych/Soc)	95 minutes	
	59 questions	

How is the MCAT scored?

When your MCAT is scored, you will receive a total of ten different scores. You'll receive a total point score for the combined test along with scores for each of the four sections. All four sections are scored between 118 points and 132 points. The lowest possible score on the MCAT is a 472 (118 × 4). The highest possible score is a 528 (132 × 4). You'll also receive a percentile score for the total and for each of the four sections to give you an idea of how you compared to others.

Your score is determined only by the number of questions you answer correctly. Incorrect answers do not count against your score. This means that answering a question incorrectly is the same as not answering it at all. I want to repeat that—incorrect answers do not count against you. Always guess!

Students are often under the misconception that the test is graded on a curve, with high scores being harder during the busiest time of the testing season. There are variations between each

MCAT that students take, and those variations are considered when your scaled score is generated. Your raw score, or the number of questions you answered correctly, is converted to the scaled score (118-132) based on the difficulty of the questions on your specific test compared to other tests. The scaled scores are not generated by looking at how other students performed.

What is a good MCAT score?

The most common question we receive from students is, "What is a good MCAT score?" It is important to remember that good MCAT scores are relative. A good score is one that increases your chances of acceptance into the medical school you want to attend. The Medical School Admissions Requirements (MSAR) and College Information Book (CIB) give prospective students an idea of what the previous year's class looks like. Use those resources to see how competitive the MCAT scores are for each school. Remember to look at more than the median score, though. The median, by definition, is the middle. Fifty percent of the class will be above that number and fifty percent below. Look at the ranges to determine your competitiveness as an applicant. Always keep in mind, though, that this test is just one part of your application. Determining the quality of your MCAT score requires you to find the average score of students accepted into those programs.

The 50th percentile for the new MCAT is a 500. If you score this, you are average. According to the AAMC[2], the mean MCAT score for applicants for 2016-2017 was 501.8. The mean MCAT score for students who were accepted to and started medical school was 508.7. Use these numbers to help guide you as you try to determine the target you are shooting for. The best answer, though, when it comes to the question of a good MCAT score, is the highest one you can get!

CHAPTER 2
How to Register for the MCAT

In this chapter, we'll cover everything you'll need to know about registering for the MCAT.

Am I eligible to take the MCAT?

To register for the MCAT, you must have the intention of utilizing your MCAT scores to apply for acceptance into medical school. You may only register for one MCAT at a time and are not eligible for registration if you've already taken the MCAT three times that year.

You may need special permission to register under certain circumstances. Check with the AAMC if you think you have a unique circumstance as to why you are taking the MCAT (i.e., you aren't planning on going to medical school).

When should I register for the MCAT?

You should register for the MCAT as soon as you can. Ideally, you want to register months in advance to ensure that you're able to take it on the day and at the location you want. Registration for the next year has historically opened mid-October of the prior year. For example, if you are hoping to take the MCAT in April of 2025, you should check the AAMC website around October 2024.

The MCAT is taken at a testing center, which has a limited number of seats for each test day. If the testing center near you is filled up and you fail to get a seat on the day you want, you may be required to take it later or travel to take the MCAT at a different location. Because you want to be as comfortable as possible during the test, it helps to be close to home, so you don't have to deal with the extra burden of traveling to the exam site.

How do I register?

Registration for the MCAT happens online, through the registration portal available on the AAMC's website. To sign up for an exam date, you need to create an account with an individual AAMC username and password.

Upon signing into the MCAT portal, you are required to fill out several forms asking for basic personal background and eligibility information. Once you complete the necessary forms, you are given a list of available testing locations. First, you need to choose the date on which you want to test. Once you choose your date, you are asked to choose the state in which you want to take the MCAT. Clicking your state takes you to a list of testing sites available on the date you chose. At this point, you should choose the site that is closest to your home or wherever you'll be on the day of the MCAT. If there are available seats, you can move forward with your registration. If there are no more available seats at that location for the date you've chosen, you'll either need to take the MCAT at a different location or move backward through the portal to choose a different testing date.

Upon choosing your MCAT site, you are prompted to submit your payment information. After submitting payment and finalizing the transaction, the portal takes you to a screen displaying receipt of your registration documenting when and where you need to report to take the exam.

Of important note, you'll also get additional information about deadlines concerning canceling and rescheduling your MCAT.

How much does the MCAT cost?

As of this writing, the initial cost of MCAT registration is $315.

Rescheduling or Canceling the MCAT

If you choose to cancel or reschedule your test day, you may incur extra costs.

If you register for the MCAT during the AAMC's Gold Period (more than one month prior to the MCAT), you'll be charged a fee of $85 to reschedule, or you will be refunded $155 if you choose to cancel. If you complete your registration three to four weeks prior to the exam, during the AAMC's Silver Period, you'll be charged a fee of $145 to reschedule. If you register during the Silver Period, you'll receive no refund in the case of cancellation. The Bronze Zone denotes the period one to two weeks before the exam, and if you register during this period, you are ineligible for both rescheduling and cancellation refunds.

	Gold Zone (deadline: 29 days prior to exam)	Silver Zone (deadline: 15 days prior to exam)	Bronze Zone (deadline: 8 days prior to exam)
Initial Registration	$315		$370
Reschedule Fee (Date or Test Center)	$90	$150	You cannot reschedule
Cancellation Refund	$155	No Cancellation Refund	
International Fee	$105		

Additionally, if you are an international student, you'll be charged a $100 processing fee for taking the MCAT outside of the US.

Is there financial aid available?

The AAMC provides a Fee Assistance Program (FAP) to help offset registration costs if you have financial limitations. Your eligibility is determined by the AAMC. You should check directly with the AAMC for the most up-to-date criteria for eligibility.

One of the biggest things to keep in mind for the FAP is that you will need to provide your parent's financial information to determine your income level. It doesn't matter if you're married or how old you are.

Once approved for the FAP, you'll receive:

– Reduced MCAT registration from $315 to $125

– Access to the book *Official Guide to the MCAT*, the AAMC practice exams, section bank and more

– Access to the Medical School Admission Requirements (MSAR) website

– AMCAS® fee waiver with up to 16 medical schools selected.

Benefits typically expire at the end of the year and you are limited to five fee assistance awards during your lifetime.

You can find out more about FAP from the AAMC at mcatbook.com/fap .

Can I get accommodations?

If you have any diagnosed disabilities or medical conditions which may require adjustments to the standard exam environment, you are encouraged to apply for accommodations. These impairments may include, but are not limited to: physical/mobility impairments, visual impairments, learning disabilities, inflammatory bowel disease, diabetes, and other medical conditions. Such impairments are accommodated with modifications such as oversized printing, extra testing time, a separate testing room, and authorization for inhalers, water, or hard candy.

If you know you need to take the MCAT under special circumstances, make sure your request for accommodations is built around your preparation schedule and allows you to have secured arrangements early enough to reserve a seat on your preferred date. Because it can take up to 60 days for accommodation requests to receive a response, applicants are advised to turn in the necessary materials as early as possible. Late requests for accommodations can result in a disruption of the registration process.

We've seen students get their accommodation requests denied at the last minute due to forgetting something. Don't let that happen to you.

How do accommodations affect my application?

If you require accommodations for the MCAT, this information does not get passed to medical schools on your application. Your score looks like every other score.

While you should get the accommodations you need to succeed on your test day, a paper published in the *Journal of the American Medical Association*[3] showed that students who received extra time for the MCAT had lower rates of passing the United States Medical Licensing Examination (USMLE®) Step examinations (also known as the "board" exams, the USMLE consists of Step 1, Step 2 CK [Clinical Knowledge], Step 2 CS [Clinical Skills], and Step 3) and lower rates of graduating medical school. USMLE Step 1 and Step 2 are taken during medical school. Step 3 is taken during residency.

How many times can I take the MCAT?

You may consider retaking the MCAT to achieve higher scores and increase your chances of getting into the school you hope to attend. The AAMC allows you to take the MCAT up to three times in any given testing year and four times during a two-consecutive-year period. You are limited to taking the MCAT seven times total over the course of your life.

While retaking the MCAT can enable you to show better scores in your medical school application, be aware that not all schools look strictly at the highest submitted score. Some schools, instead, look at the most recent score or the average of all scores. We'll cover more about retaking the MCAT later in this book.

Can I cancel or reschedule the MCAT?

If you register early enough, you can cancel or reschedule your MCAT any time before two weeks prior to the MCAT. As previously pointed out, the cost of your cancellation or rescheduling fees will be determined by the Zone in which you registered. If you registered within the Gold Zone, for example, you'll receive a partial refund upon canceling your reservation. If you register during the Silver Zone, you'll still be able to cancel your MCAT date but will have to pay a higher rescheduling fee than those who registered within the Gold Zone.

Because there is no option to cancel within two weeks of your MCAT date, you are not eligible to cancel if you registered during the Bronze Zone.

If you don't cancel in time, you may think about taking the MCAT and voiding it, just to give you the experience of going to the testing center and checking in.

CHAPTER 3
WHEN SHOULD I TAKE THE MCAT

When you take the MCAT can have a huge impact on your application to medical school. Don't let taking it at the wrong time prevent you from acceptance to medical school the first time you apply.

When is the MCAT offered?

The MCAT is typically offered between January and September every year. You can always find the most current MCAT schedule at mcatbook.com/mcatdates.

What classes do I need to take the MCAT?

Before talking about scheduling your MCAT, let's first talk about what classes you should have under your belt to prepare for it.

Planning your schedule to cover every subject you need to take before the MCAT can be confusing enough. To complicate things even further, you need to sort through the required classes for each of the medical schools you are interested in and make sure that you're also taking those, in addition to the right classes to help you prepare for the MCAT.

What classes should you take before taking the MCAT, and how much weight should you give MCAT prep when determining your schedule?

The AAMC recommends a year each of chemistry, organic chemistry, physics, and biology, and a semester each of psychology, sociology, and biochemistry. If a med school is telling you that you should take other specific classes, then you need to make sure you follow those specific guidelines as well.

The course load to be the most prepared for the MCAT is intense. Some students look for ways to cut corners by not taking all the recommended courses, or even taking the MCAT after they have graduated, so they don't have to worry about squeezing in all the classes and the prep during a "normal" timeframe.

Biology is, by far, the most tested subject on the MCAT, followed by psychology. Sometimes students will feel confident in their knowledge of sociology and forgo that recommended semester. However, the MCAT will be looking for specific technical definitions of words which are covered in a semester of sociology. For that reason, it's worth taking each recommendation seriously.

See your advisor

If you have access to an advisor, now is the time to see him or her. Your advisor will typically have a timeline based on your school's specific courses that are available. This specific knowledge will hopefully give you the best idea of when you'll be able to take the MCAT.

Are there any "hidden" prereqs?

The MCAT tests biology heavily; one year is more than likely not enough to cover the material you will find on the test. Specifically, the MCAT tests "biology of the small" (cells, organelles, sub-cellular structures, and pathway). This includes the anatomy and physiology of the human body, but it's not expected that you take those classes for the MCAT. We recommend completing a second year of biology, focusing on one mid to upper-level cell bio course and one mid to upper-level molecular genetics course, or something along those lines.

A humanities class like English, philosophy, or history can help you build critical reasoning and reading skills. At its core, the MCAT is a reading test covering science subjects. Fitting in as many non-science classes as possible will help you master the Critical Analysis and Reasoning Skills section of the MCAT. The CARS section is almost always the hardest section of the MCAT for most students.

Can I self-study a subject?

If your hands are tied, and you have no option but to take the MCAT prior to completing all the classes we've suggested, it is possible to self-study a subject to gain enough mastery of the material to do well on the MCAT.

Don't expect to do it all on your own though—there are limits. While you are studying for the MCAT, don't try to self-study more than one semester of coursework. Self-studying a semester's worth of material while preparing to take the MCAT is not an easy or fun thing to do, but it can be done successfully. If you need to do one semester of sociology, do it. One semester of physics, good luck. Two semesters? Don't even think about it.

If you find yourself in a situation where you have a few semesters of suggested coursework to complete before taking the MCAT, you should consider waiting to take the test. The amount of material that you'll need to study is simply too large, and the most likely outcome is a poor score and the need to retake the test anyway. Rushing to take the MCAT may help you apply to a school this cycle, but it may prevent you from getting an acceptance because of a low score.

It is always better to take the MCAT when you are ready, not when you think you must take it.

Are there any subjects I can skip?

There aren't many shortcuts in life, but there may be a little wiggle room on the MCAT. Organic chemistry, the great gatekeeper of the premed world, is underrepresented on the MCAT. As a prereq, you are expected to take two semesters, but if you need to take the MCAT before you get the second semester under your belt, you should be okay. The same goes for the second semester of physics.

How am I expected to know everything?

The test itself can be very overwhelming, considering there is far more material covered on it than on any test you've previously taken. The MCAT is a shallow test, though, and does not dig very deep into the subjects on which it touches. When taking the MCAT, you won't have to delve into topics the way you would for the final exam of a semester-long course.

It will look like a lot, but adequate preparation will make it easier. Once you've taken the prerequisite courses and started to prepare for the test, ask yourself which subjects make you feel the most insecure. Review your diagnostic or full-length test to see where you are struggling. Start your preparation by reviewing those subjects. Building confidence around the topics you're most uncomfortable with will help you maximize your score on the MCAT.

When should I take it?

The most common (and recommended) time to take the MCAT is during the spring of the calendar year before you want to start medical school. For example, if you're planning to start medical school in August of 2025, then take the MCAT in April or May of

2024. Applications for the 2025 starting class open in May and June. This will enable you to have your scores in before you apply so you can judge whether you should delay your application a year to better prepare for the MCAT. If your score isn't bad enough to delay a full year, it will still give you adequate time to retake the test during the application cycle. This will delay your application being complete, but it's not a deal breaker for admissions.

Make sure you understand the application timeline as you plan for taking the MCAT. It is important to note that it takes roughly one month for your scores to be returned. This means after taking the test, you'll have to wait thirty days before you know if your scores are strong enough to get you into the school to which you're applying. Most schools won't review your application at all until they've received your MCAT scores, so you want to leave enough time to receive and submit the best possible score.

Remember, when it comes to applying for medical school, earlier is better. Most medical schools accept students on a rolling admissions basis. The later your application is complete, the harder your chances of getting accepted. Don't think about your application in terms of, "When is the last day I can apply?" but rather, "How can I prepare myself to apply as soon as possible?"

One other thing to keep in mind is that even if you are planning on taking the MCAT later, it is still highly recommended to submit your application early so it can be verified. If you wait for your scores, your application will be even more delayed. You don't have to wait for your test scores. The longer you wait to submit, the longer it will be for your application to be verified—even if you submit and register for a new MCAT test.

Am I ready to take the MCAT?

Knowing if you are ready to take the MCAT comes down to how well you prepared. If you've followed all our advice, taken almost all (if not all) of your prereqs, taken many full-length practice tests (simulating a real testing environment) and you are scoring well, then you are probably ready to take the test.

If you have not taken the time to sit down for a full eight-hour day to take a practice test, but instead did one or two sections at a time, and have assumed your overall score based on those scores, then you are not ready for the real MCAT.

If your scores are where you want them to be, with some consistency on your full-lengths, then you are ready to take the MCAT.

Being prepared to take the MCAT on time will require planning, but if you understand different pieces of the overall puzzle, you'll be on track to take the test at a time where you can score well and have it not delay your application.

Don't Take it Too Soon

The MCAT is typically only valid for three years. There may be some schools that want an MCAT score from only two years ago. This means that if you plan on taking some gap years to do research or travel, you may not want to take the MCAT during the normal timeframe.

If you're only planning on one gap year, you may be okay. If you're thinking about two gap years, think about what might happen if you don't get into medical school your first time applying. With two gap years and a failed application, you'll need to take the MCAT again. Based on this, if you're planning on taking two gap years, I would recommend you delay taking the MCAT for at least one year.

Nontraditional Student Advice

If you're a nontraditional student, the advice is mostly the same. You'll need to make sure you have the prereqs under your belt to have a solid foundation of the material covered on the MCAT. If your prereqs were many years ago, you might consider retaking them, even if you did well originally. This will be an individual decision that each student will need to make.

One thing to know about prereqs: Some schools will require classes taken within five years, and some ten. As you do your research into schools, give them a call to discuss your situation and see what specific recommendations they have for you. One of the most challenging parts of applying to medical school is knowing that every school has different requirements.

Postbac Programs

If it's been a long time since you've taken your prereqs, or if you haven't taken any yet, you may want to look into a formal postbac program which can help you get the prereqs you need and get you prepared to take the MCAT. There are year-long, intensive programs, or programs that are two years long. Check the AAMC postbac directory at https://apps.aamc.org/postbac.

CHAPTER 4
HOW TO STUDY FOR THE MCAT

Where to start

As soon as you realize you need to take this big, scary test to get into medical school, you need to start by familiarizing yourself with the basics. Before going to a prep company, taking prep courses, or planning your practice tests, you want to get as much information from the AAMC as possible.

Luckily, the AAMC offers an MCAT test prep book called *The Official Guide to the MCAT Exam,* an up-to-date resource by the writers of the test. The book outlines how the exam was compiled and will help you familiarize yourself with the structure of the MCAT. It also provides many practice questions to aid you in developing a course of study as you begin to prepare for taking the test. The AAMC's guide is readily available on Amazon for around $30.

The best way to start your preparation is to work through the AAMC book from cover to cover. While the book itself is very dry and reading the whole thing will be an exhausting endeavor, doing so, in combination with reading this book, will let you know exactly what to expect on the exam and give you a strong idea of how to plan your preparation.

The MCAT Podcast

The MCAT Podcast is a free resource that you can add to your phone and listen to while cooking, cleaning, working out, or driving. Check it out at themcatpodcast.com.

Are there any other books I should buy?

Any bookstore, social media platform, or online premed forum will recommend various MCAT preparation books. Because there are so many out there, it can be intimidating to figure out which ones you really need. To make matters even more complicated, anxiety and the desire to do well can often lead you to make impulsive choices when buying books and amassing a huge library in the hope that more information will help you do better on the test.

You want to remember that a tall stack of books does not necessarily translate into a good MCAT score. Efficiently utilizing these books is the only true method for success on the exam.

In reality, one set of books, used properly, will provide you with enough information to prepare adequately for the exam. While there is no magic set of books that will unlock the secrets to a perfect score (despite what people on the internet might claim), having several produced by a reputable company will help you prepare for the MCAT. This will save you time and money along with enabling you to stop shopping around and start focusing on studying.

When browsing for MCAT prep material, make sure to look only for books published by companies that work with live human beings. We're obviously partial to Next Step Test Prep books, which are available through Amazon. Here at Next Step, we produce our books by working with experienced professionals in the medical education field. There is a certain kind of institutional knowledge acquired by doing so—which cannot be replicated and translates into much better test prep material. This is not to say that prep books published by other companies are bad, but there is a noticeable difference in quality from books produced through working with experienced professionals.

When looking for books, keep in mind that practice will be the key to getting strong MCAT scores. Many books, like Next Step's MCAT Series, include questions designed to help you practice as you read through it. Finding a book that enables you to do this will simultaneously provide you with necessary information and help you to retain it through helpful practice testing. In fact, Next Step's books have a number of questions to help you get into the mindset of taking the MCAT and not just trying to memorize facts.

Ultimately, you want to remind yourself that books are only helpful if used properly. Often, students are tempted to read through their books very quickly and superficially, expecting to get great scores. Make sure that, whichever books you buy, you read them more thoroughly and carefully than any textbook you would have purchased for a class. Think of your prep books the way a musician thinks about their sheet music. When performing a musical score, a professional musician can perform the music and focus on the conductor because they've already mastered the composition. To achieve the best possible scores, you want to have mastery of the material outlined in your prep books.

If you are struggling with one specific section of the MCAT, you may want to consider section-specific books. A good section practice book will give you an outline of the necessary material in addition to practice tests and sample questions based solely around that subject.

For example, many of us spend so much time reviewing the science material that we often feel very intimidated by the Critical Analysis and Reasoning Skills (CARS) section of the test. If you feel this way, you may want to pick up a book focusing strictly on the CARS section of the exam. These books will provide you with dozens of sample passages to complete and give you in-depth breakdowns of your answers to help prepare you for the CARS section of the MCAT. Like all of these preparation materials, whether or not you need such a book depends on how prepared you feel to handle those sections on the test.

Next Step offers eleven books, ranging from section specific content review to strategy to questions. You can find all of Next Step's MCAT books on Amazon.

Do I need to take a diagnostic test?

You may have been told by a friend (or read on that notoriously bad premed forum) that diagnostic MCAT tests are not important. The common misconception is that these tests are designed only to scare you into buying a test preparation package. However, you'll want to take a diagnostic test either right before or when you start to prepare for the MCAT. Doing so will give you an idea of where your strengths and weaknesses lie so that you can begin your preparation with a good idea of where to focus.

Luckily, most diagnostic tests are available for no cost through most test prep companies. Next Step offers a free diagnostic and a free full-length exam when you sign up. A diagnostic test is often similar to the MCAT itself, but not necessarily a recreation of the exam experience. It probably won't be a full eight-hour test, but is structured in the same format as the real MCAT and simulates the difficulty of the actual exam. While many diagnostic tests are only half as long as the real MCAT, they are effectively designed to provide you with an initial analysis around which to plan your course of study.

A good MCAT diagnostic test can predict how well you would do on the real test if you were to take it that day. For this reason, you want to take your diagnostic as early as you possibly can. You don't need to wait until after you've taken all of the required prerequisites before signing up for a diagnostic test. Going in without having prepared will give you an honest assessment of how much time your preparation will take.

The amount of time you need to put into your MCAT preparation is different than the amount of time other students need to put into theirs. Taking a diagnostic will give you an idea of what your version of preparation will look like. If you score within the top 10% of your diagnostic test, for example, you will have a different course of action than someone who scores around the 50th percentile. After taking a diagnostic, you'll be able to develop realistic goals for scoring on the MCAT and a working plan to achieve those goals.

Ready to take a diagnostic? Next Step has a free diagnostic that also gives you access to a free full-length MCAT practice test. Go to mcatbook.com/freetest to get access to the tests.

Are there any other prep materials?

In addition to the options listed above, there are many preparation products and services that can help you supplement your chosen method of study. While they aren't as vital as diagnostic testing, practice tests, and rigorous study, the wide selection of available materials might be helpful during the process of preparation.

Many companies working in MCAT preparation, for example, offer a resource known as "Qbanks" in addition to the practice test and prep course services. Qbanks are essentially large databases of sample questions compiled to help you study. Different from practice tests (they are not structured in the form of a test), Qbanks provide you with a resource you can continually return to familiarize yourself with the types of questions presented on the exam. Many students use Qbanks to develop practice tests for themselves, and some MCAT prep companies even utilize Qbanks to offer customized, on-demand mini-tests. Unlike traditional MCAT prep books, Qbanks are offered exclusively online and can be accessed from your laptop or mobile devices so that you can easily work your way through MCAT test prep questions on-the-go.

The AAMC MCAT Section Bank is another resource that will be extremely valuable to your preparation. Providing over 300 discrete and passage-based practice questions, the Section Bank helps you test yourself in each subject covered on the test. Available through the AAMC website for only $45, the Section Bank gives you the opportunity to "start" each section ten times before your subscription expires. Because it allows you to take practice tests online, it gives you the opportunity to experience the testing environment and review your results immediately so you can improve your future score.

Full-Length MCAT Practice Tests

Do I need to take full-length practice tests?

It cannot be stressed enough: when it comes to MCAT preparation, taking and reviewing practice tests is the best way to increase your potential to do well on the test. Whether you're looking to get a strong, mid-range score or work your way into the upper rankings, you'll want to take practice tests to perform your best.

Even if you performed very well on your diagnostic tests, MCAT practice tests have much more in common with the actual exam. Taking practice tests will give you the opportunity to reinforce your testing skills, review the necessary information, and glean valuable insight into where you can continue to improve your score. They'll also give you the stamina it takes to sit for almost eight hours while taking a test.

Next Step offers bundles of full-length MCAT practice exams which give reliable scores very close to what you will experience on the real MCAT, as well as the AAMC full-length exams. Use the discount code "MCATBOOK" to save 10%.

How many practice tests should I take?

While there is almost no limit to the number of practice tests you can take, you want to take at least three practice tests during your preparation process. As of this publishing, the AAMC has released three official, scored full-length practice tests for the new MCAT. You should be sure to take every practice test the AAMC releases. If, in the future, the organization makes more practice tests available, be sure that you take advantage of these as well. Because the AAMC is the developer and administer of the MCAT, taking their tests will give you valuable insight into the nature of the exam during any given year. You cannot consider yourself an adequately prepared MCAT student if you have not, at the bare minimum, done the official AAMC practice tests.

Additionally, it is recommended that you take two or three additional full-length MCAT practice tests. A well prepared MCAT student will have taken a total of five or six practice exams before showing up on their testing day. Unfortunately, many students show up on test day without taking any, and it shows when they get their score back.

In extreme cases, you might consider extending the number of practice tests to as many as ten if you're having trouble improving your score. This is a good idea if you struggle with standardized testing and perform poorly either on the MCAT or other tests like the SAT. Unfortunately, taking more than ten practice tests will most likely result in diminishing returns. If this is the case for you, review the practice tests you've taken, assess the problems you faced, and spend your time studying as opposed to taking more tests.

When should I take practice tests?

MCAT full-length practice tests are intended to get you in the habit of taking the exam, so you should still take some within the few weeks leading up to your test date.

As with the MCAT itself, however, knowing when you're prepared to take practice tests will be dependent on your situation. There is no one-size-fits-all answer, as you may be less prepared for a practice test than other students.

Make sure that you take these tests at the point in your preparation process when they are most useful to you. This means that the best time to take practice exams is while you still have time to review the results and use them to assist you with your MCAT preparation. Don't save practice tests for the days leading up to the exam, as you'll risk scaring yourself and making the process unproductive.

Where do I buy full-length MCAT practice tests?

The official AAMC MCAT practice test can be purchased through the organization's website. Each sample test costs roughly $25 and is released at a different point in the testing season. Next Step offers "bundle" packages which provide access to four, six, or even ten full-length practice tests that will help you prepare for the MCAT. Use the discount code "MCATBOOK" to save 10% off Next Step full-length exams.

How do I fit practice tests into my prep schedule?

The best part about practice tests is that they are full-length exams, designed to simulate the test day. Because you are responsible for taking them on your own, however, it will require some discipline and scheduling on your part. You will, after all, need to administer the test yourself. You'll have to set aside a full day and strictly stick to the timing, giving yourself the exact same length of break permitted during the real MCAT.

To do this, plan a day where you can be at the library by 8 AM and start the test by 8:30 AM. Keep in mind that this is when you'll be required to report to the actual MCAT on testing day and sticking to the schedule while taking practice tests helps prepare you for the exam.

As mentioned previously, make sure you are taking practice tests during the weeks leading up to the MCAT. Set aside one day a week to spend at the library testing yourself. The idea is to get as much test-like practice as possible in the weeks before the exam itself.

It will be most beneficial for you to take the AAMC practice exams during the few weeks prior to your test date (see Last Minute MCAT Tips chapter later in this book). Because these tests are created by the same people who wrote the MCAT, it will be most like the actual test. Scheduling yourself to take practice exams during your final preparation stages will help you to best prepare for your testing day. Make sure to save the AAMC's unscored practice test for the final week, as this will give you the experience of testing without providing a score that could freak you out at the last minute.

Take the AAMC's scored versions during the two weeks prior to that.

How do I review my practice tests?

When reviewing the results of your practice exams, start by looking at the questions that made you the most nervous during the test. At this point, return to your notes and study guides to figure out why these questions scared you and how you should approach them in the future.

Your practice tests should be used the same way your diagnostic tests were, as a kind of "thermometer" to take note of problems you need to solve. This is why it's so helpful to take multiple tests. If you're taking practice tests six or eight weeks before your MCAT, you have plenty of time to review the necessary information.

Remember, during the last few weeks of MCAT prep, it is impossible to review everything. If you attempt to review everything, you'll ultimately end up reviewing nothing. Casually skimming the MCAT will lead you nowhere; instead, focus on the topics you are most uncom fortable with and chip away at your insecurities about them.

We have a sample spreadsheet explaining how to best review the MCAT, so you get an idea of what you need to review. Go to http://mcatbook.com/spreadsheet to download it now.

Do I need to take an MCAT prep course?

As you start your MCAT preparation, you may be wondering about the necessity of a prep course. Is it necessary or can you self-study?

Like every aspect of the preparation process, there are pros and cons to MCAT prep courses. Self-study will definitely work for some of you, a course is going to be a good fit for many, and one-on-one tutoring will be the best option for others. After taking a diagnostic test and assessing your study habits, you should have a good idea of the type of study that will best help you through the preparation process.

For example, if you are someone who is naturally very good at standardized testing, and are disciplined, then you probably don't need to take a course. A dedicated self-study block of time will probably get you where you need to be regarding MCAT scores. However, if you are a person that feels like the rigor and commitment of a prep course would benefit you, then you should take one.

After all, the benefits of a prep course are the same as learning in any structured course environment. You'll have strict deadlines, assignments, and practice test dates that will help you to stay on track and take responsibility for learning the necessary material within a certain timeframe. Many test prep courses will provide a massive quantity of books, tests, and videos to help you learn and prepare for the exam. This can be extremely helpful to students who find that they lose focus when they must read, study, and seek out information on their own.

However, some MCAT prep courses come with a high price tag. With some courses costing upwards of $2,500 or more, prep courses are a large financial investment. To choose a prep course that is worth the money you'll spend, make sure to find one that will be a benefit to your preparation process.

How do I choose a prep course?

If you have decided to take a prep course, when you start searching for one you'll want to be sure it is going to be as valuable as possible to your preparation process. There are so many courses out there; it can be tough to find the right one.

First, make sure you enroll in an MCAT focused course. While this seems obvious, there are many prep courses designed to help students better themselves in the general practice of standardized testing. This means students who are enrolled in those courses are not receiving instruction on how to take the MCAT specifically, but instead on how to do better on tests such as the SAT, GRE, and others. This may be helpful for some test-takers out there but your time is valuable when preparing for the MCAT. You want to make sure you're using your study time in the most efficient manner possible.

Second, be sure to enroll in a course taught by experts. Signing up for a course taught by someone who is well-versed and up-to-date in MCAT preparation will be much more of a benefit to you than someone who has been appointed to teach without much experience in taking the class. Contact the venue offering the course and research their instructors online to ensure that you're signing up for a strong and beneficial prep course. You'll also want to know how the teachers are trained to teach the material. Just because they may have received a high score on the MCAT, it doesn't automatically mean they will be good at teaching you the material.

Last, and most important, make sure the course you're signing up for is one taught in a way that will most benefit your preparation process. If the course is taught through a series of lectures, for example, and you're a traditional premed, still taking classes, it probably won't be right for you because you've already sat through the lectures recently. You most likely will want to take a course based on small group instruction and "hands-on" interaction with the prep material.

The most important factor in choosing a test prep course is knowing if they'll provide you with sufficient practice tests to prepare you for taking the exam. Practice, after all, is the number one way to acclimate yourself with testing, and it provides valuable information about where you need to go back and review more. While you'll have a variety of options regarding which courses to take, one that does not prepare you with practice tests is not one which will benefit you in the long-run.

Next Step's MCAT course meets and exceeds all the criteria listed here. It's an online, self-paced course with some of the top experts in MCAT prep teaching the material and holding live office hours several times a week. You'll get access to videos which help you master the material you need to master. You'll get every Next Step book and access to all of Next Step's top-ranked, full-length practice exams. Find out more at nextstepmcat.com/course and use the code "MCATBOOK" to save $50 off the rice of Next Step's MCAT Course.

Online or in-person?

Choosing to prepare using an online prep course versus a course taught at a brick and mortar location is a decision based on your needs, lifestyle and learning habits. If you are too busy to commit to another class where you must show up on a weekly basis, you might opt to take the course online. This will allow you to complete the work during whatever time is best for you to do so. Some online courses are live, while some are at your own pace; make sure you have enough self-awareness to know what you need so you can get the most out of your prep time.

As pointed out above, however, taking the class in-person will give you solid deadlines and the opportunity to interact with professors face-to-face. While this is a great way to help certain personalities prepare for the exam, choosing your course style will take some decision making on your part. If you're concerned about getting that interaction with an instructor, in-person isn't the only way to go. Next Step's MCAT course has the most live office hours of any online MCAT prep course.

Should I find a study group?

A great way to prepare for the MCAT is to approach study as a collaborative activity. In fact, forming study groups is one of the best and most effective ways to prepare for the exam. It is generally easy to put one together and costs nothing. If you and your classmates utilize each other's strengths in the right ways, you can work as a group to overcome individual deficiencies in each of your knowledge bases.

As effective as assembling a study group can be, it can also present a problem: you must pick and choose who you want to spend time studying with. The biggest mistake students often make is trying to surround themselves with only the smartest people they know. When putting together your group, however, you want to find individuals who have strengths and weaknesses which complement one another. For example, if you have a strong working knowledge of organic chemistry but have a tough time in psychology, you ideally want to get someone in your study group who is the opposite of you. The reason for this is if someone lacks knowledge in a subject where you are confident, you'll need to spend time teaching this subject to that person.

Spending time teaching other people is one of the best ways to learn more about the topic and reinforce the subjects you already know and understand. After months of teaching organic chemistry to another person, you'll have a strengthened confidence around the subject that will help you tackle it during the exam. At the same time, other students will be teaching you about their strengths, forming a mutually beneficial group relationship.

During medical school, it is commonplace for students to form study groups to work their way through dense amounts of material. Starting a study group during your MCAT prep will prepare you for the collaborative nature of study in medical school.

If you would like help finding a study group, go to mcatstudygroups.com.

Is a private tutor worth it?

In addition to study groups and self-study, you may want to consider one-on-one tutoring to prepare for the MCAT. There is no doubt tutoring can help everybody, so it's never a bad thing to do. Simply put, some students find they can prepare better for the exam through other means of studying, such as tutoring.

If you find yourself struggling to get an adequate score, you might be someone who will benefit from private tutoring. If your scores are within the 10th or 20th MCAT percentiles, self-study and prep courses won't provide you with the structure and attention you need while preparing for the exam. Again, prep courses focus on those achieving average scores. One-on-one tutoring will be customized to help you prepare for those subjects you're having the most trouble with and will ultimately be the key to help you reach higher scores on the MCAT.

Tutoring also works extremely well for those students who are aiming to perform within the highest percentiles of the exam. If you already have a 513 from a previous MCAT and are still looking to perform higher on the exam, private tutoring is your best option. The standard prep courses won't be effective in helping you to achieve scores this high, as they cater to a broader base of students. One-on-one instruction is something you will want to seek out. In this case, make sure you find and hire a tutor who can provide you with the necessary information and guidance.

Also, if you're a nontraditional student, you might find that private tutoring is a great way to reintegrate yourself into the process of studying for this massive exam. If you have been out of school for a long time, you will benefit from the custom guidance that one-on-one tutoring provides.

If you don't identify with any of the students listed above but are finding that self-study and prep courses are still leaving you feeling overwhelmed and lost, private tutoring will be the best possible help in your situation. The attention, focus, and customized plan of study may be exactly what you need to make sure the next MCAT test you take is your last one.

While one-on-one tutoring continuously proves to be the most effective method of test preparation, it does have the downside of generally being more expensive than other forms of study. Because study groups are free and prep courses are usually less expensive, it can be financially easier to choose one of those options when preparing for the MCAT. However, if you can afford to invest in the entirely customizable experience which a private tutor provides, this route is highly recommended. You may be surprised to learn that a private tutor from Next Step does not cost much more than a full prep course from some of the other companies. As of this writing, 24 hours of one-on-one tutoring from Next Step is only $400 more than a live-online course from one of the other big test prep companies. For the extra cost (less than $17 an hour), wouldn't you like to have someone personally looking out for exactly what you need to do to prepare the best way possible for the MCAT?

If you're interested in learning more about how Next Step tutoring can help you prepare for the MCAT, schedule a consultation call at mcatbook.com/consult and let them know you read this book. You'll also save $50 off any of their tutoring packages by using the link above and mentioning the book.

Common preparation pitfalls

Students make different kinds of mistakes when preparing for the MCAT. There are those who buy way too many books and get lost under the pile, there are those who don't buy enough books, and there are those who just don't use their books properly. Once you have your preparation materials ready to go and your preparation process is well underway, there are a few mistakes which you want to be sure to avoid.

Focusing on just the content

For one, you want to make sure that you take enough practice exams. Because practice exams can be so overwhelming, many students make the mistake of taking too few or no practice exams. They get lazy and either don't take practice tests or don't take their practice tests as seriously as they should. Simulating the test day will be extremely beneficial, and you want to make sure you treat it like the real experience. This means sitting down for the full (almost) eight hours. No music. No phones. No distractions.

Not reviewing full-length exams

When you take practice exams, don't be the student who makes the mistake of not fully reviewing your test—including both wrong and right answers. While you want to take the test to see what your score is, practice tests will only help you as much as you allow. To improve your MCAT score, make sure you carefully analyze each test after you take it. Spend anywhere from eight to eighteen hours doing a careful autopsy of every single question. While this might be a boring and time consuming process, it is incredibly productive and will enable you to understand exactly what went wrong during your testing process. Instead of just testing for the score and moving onto the next test, use your score to learn everything you can about your strengths and weaknesses.

Not having a solid foundation of the material

Treat your MCAT books the same way. The information in them needs to be mastered before you move on. While it is easy to skim the book and feel like you have an adequate understanding of the material, you won't learn what you need to unless you spend time truly understanding the content within each book. After studying each chapter, give yourself a two or three day break before returning to and reviewing it.

Not finding the right study habit for you

With YouTube, Instagram and other social media channels, it's very easy to see what other people are doing to prepare for the MCAT. You can find many resources from students who scored very well on the MCAT—some even offer solid advice on how you should study.

Unfortunately, their study habits might not work well for you.

You need to understand your strengths and weaknesses when it comes to studying. You need to maximize your strengths. When it comes to the MCAT, you don't have enough time to work on your weaknesses—a process which can take years.

Taking the test too soon

Lastly, and most importantly, make sure that you don't rush into taking the MCAT before you're ready. Often, students will waste valuable time taking an exam they aren't ready for, at which point they have to wait a month before getting their scores back. Rushing the exam can be detrimental to your timeline; don't make that mistake.

How do I manage stress while preparing for the MCAT?

The MCAT preparation process can be one of the most stressful times in your academic life. Because you have so much going on while preparing to take the MCAT, it is important that you understand how to reduce the amount of stress you encounter. After all, stress is a physiological condition that has a vast impact on your cognitive processes. Being able to destress will ultimately increase your chances of performing better on the test.

When preparing for the MCAT, you should be getting exercise every day. Daily aerobic exercise greatly reduces your stress levels, increases the positive hormones running around in your body, and has an enormous positive impact on your brain's performance. Studies show that people who exercise perform higher on tests based on IQ and memory; you want to make sure you're working out if you plan on taking the MCAT seriously. Take your dog for a walk, play some soccer, go to the gym—do whatever it takes to get your body moving and your pulse rate up.

While it may sound silly, mindfulness meditation is another method of stress management that will help you through the MCAT preparation process. Essentially, you want to make sure you're slowing down for fifteen or twenty minutes each day. This will help you to mitigate the amount of stress you're going through and, like exercise, will enable your brain to work at a better rate. There are plenty of techniques for meditating; try some out and see which one works best for you. When combined with exercise, meditation will aid your cognitive functions in operating at their highest possible level.

Additionally, it helps to familiarize yourself with the procedures that take place on the day of testing. This will prevent you from being thrown off by the events of test day so you can feel at ease when you show up for the exam.

For example, visiting the location ahead of time will help you prepare for traveling to the MCAT testing site. When you register for the MCAT, the AAMC notifies you of the exact location you should report to in order to take the test. It may sound ridiculous, but visiting the test site ahead of time will save you a ton of stress on the day of the MCAT. Traveling to the location, parking in the parking lot and finding the entrances will give you a good idea of how long it will take you to get there and how you should go about entering the building.

CHAPTER 5
RETAKING THE MCAT

How many people retake?

Because the MCAT is such an exhausting and intimidating test to prepare for and take, most of us never want to go through the process more than once. However, you may find yourself in the position of having to test multiple times. While this can be anxiety inducing, it is important to know that many students retake the test, so you are not alone.

In fact, around 10% of test-takers retake the test a second time every year[4]. A smaller amount of people (less than 1%) take it three or more times. Considering the fact that tens of thousands of people take the MCAT every year, that means there are quite a few students who retake the MCAT. The need to retake is not something people like to advertise, which is why you may think the numbers are lower.

Should I retake?

Deciding whether or not to retake the MCAT can be a tough decision —one that requires you to think about your past score rationally. Instead of scheduling your retake the moment you open up the AAMC portal and view your score, take some time to consider whether or not it will truly be beneficial. Talk to your peers, family, professors, and advisors about the possibility of retaking the test before jumping right back into another massive investment of time and financial resources.

You need to consider a number of different factors before deciding whether or not to retake the test. There are risks involved, after all. You need to think about your current schedule. Are you taking a bigger course load now, since you weren't originally planning to retake the MCAT? Are you working more, or involved in other extracurriculars?

While the goal of retaking the MCAT is to get a higher score than when you took it the first time (roughly three points higher, as a rule of thumb), many test takers do the same or worse when they retake the exam. According to the AAMC[5], about one-third of the students who start with a score in the 88th percentile (32 on the old exam, 511/512 on the new exam) receive a score equal to or lower upon taking the test a second time.

If you're able to get a higher score on your second or third time taking the test, medical schools will most likely be impressed by your ability to prepare for the retake and perform better after rigorous study. However, if you do worse on the second test than you did on the first, you might inhibit your chances of acceptance by giving the admissions committee the idea you do not have a firm grasp on the material.

Before retaking the MCAT, it helps to assess your score in terms of what your goals are. Is it imperative that you get into a so-called "top-tier" school? Is it possible for you to apply to schools where your score is more in line with their average student scores? Are you willing to consider going to a Caribbean medical school instead of a school in the states or Canada? Are you hoping to balance a weak GPA with a stellar MCAT score?

Ultimately, you'll want to consider why it is so crucial for you to become a doctor. Since you can make a living in the healthcare industry any number of ways other than practicing as a physician, taking a personal inventory will help you decide whether or not to retake the test. If, in your mind, you know you need to be a physician, but you don't have the score to get into medical school, then you should retake the MCAT and make sure you are adequately prepared to earn a better score.

If you are disappointed in yourself for needing to retake the MCAT, or you are questioning your goals because of a low score, remember: the MCAT is not a direct reflection of your potential to be a great doctor.

How should I prep for a retake?

If you decide to retake the MCAT, the first thing you need to do is get in touch with people who can help you outline a plan to prepare for your next exam. Review the Medical School Admissions Requirements (MSAR) database and College Information Book (CIB) for the MCAT ranges of students accepted to the schools you are interested in attending. While looking at ranges will not change your situation, you may be able to glean valuable information about how your score will be assessed in relationship to your GPA and other components of the application.

Don't just look at the median MCAT score, though. That number is too broad, with 50% of the class higher than that number, and more importantly, 50% of the class below it. When looking at the MSAR, look at the ranges, ideally the 10-90th percentile range (the MSAR gives you median, 25-75th percentile, and 10-90th percentile). If your MCAT score is below the 10th percentile, then you may have a hard time getting into that school with your current score.

Additionally, make an appointment with your premed advisor at your school. They can look at your MCAT scores and GPA and get an idea of how you should prep for your retake.

Ultimately, preparing for a retake will require a significant investment of your time. The amount of time you'll have to prepare depends on how much you want to improve and how much time you have before retaking the exam. Review your MCAT scores, take a number of practice tests, and take note of the subjects in which you need to improve. Develop a course of action for studying and building your confidence in these subjects.

If you didn't use a prep course before, now may be the time to look into one. Next Step offers their MCAT Course which includes several live office hours every week.

If you did use a course, you might be able to get a refund and use that money for one-on-one tutoring from Next Step.

Common pitfalls for retakes

The biggest mistake students make when preparing for their MCAT retake is continuing the bad study habits that got them an insufficient score in the first place. Take a hard look at what your habits are, where you gloss over material that needs more attention, and what you can do to make sure you're grasping the information you need to grasp. Self-awareness is key to ensuring you make the strides necessary to improve your score.

Sometimes, for example, when preparing for the MCAT, students assume that taking practice tests will be a surefire way to help them raise their score on the exam. It is important to remember that, while beneficial, taking practice tests does not automatically raise your MCAT score. Instead, these tests are a way of assessing where your strengths and weaknesses are so you can figure out how to emphasize your study in the subjects you need to work on the most. Think of your practice tests and your previous experience with the MCAT as a way of taking your temperature. Like taking one's temperature, this information can only be used to diagnose the problem and find ways to fix it. Take a look at your practice scores, your official score, and use the analysis provided to plan a course of study that will help you to perform better in the future.

Another huge pitfall for students is rushing a retake, trying to squeeze in the last test of the MCAT testing year. You may be doing yourself more harm than good if you are trying to take the test as a way to help with your current application cycle, without actually making sure you are ready to take it. You may need to do some reflection and plan to take more time off to prepare for your MCAT retake and apply to medical school the following year.

CHAPTER 6
VOIDING THE MCAT

The ability to void the MCAT can be a blessing and a curse. We've heard every reason possible why a student voided or didn't void his or her exam. We'll cover the ins and outs of voiding the MCAT here.

What happens when I void an exam?

At the end of your MCAT test day, you have the option to void your exam score. Choosing to do so is the only way to prevent scores from being recorded in your testing history. As opposed to not showing up, voiding your MCAT will not be reported to medical schools during your application process.

However, a voided MCAT does count as one of your three attempts for the testing year. If you choose to void the MCAT, you will only have two more chances to take the MCAT during the given testing year.

Using the actual MCAT as a practice test

There are students who purposefully go into a test knowing they're going to void it. This is nothing more than an overpriced practice test. If somebody said to you they'd give you a practice exam, but it's going to cost you $300, would you even buy it? Of course, not.

Use practice tests from Next Step, which cost less for ten exams versus $300 for the real MCAT. Voiding the MCAT does not cost anything extra.

If you're in a situation where you're too close to the test date to reschedule the exam, this may be the only time we'd recommend taking the test, knowing that you are going to void it.

Unlike a real practice test, when you void your MCAT, the test isn't scored, so you don't get any true feedback other than having gone through the process.

Deciding to Void in the Middle of Your Test Day

The mechanics of voiding it is that it's done at the end of the day. If you're going to leave in the middle of the test, they're going to score your test. To void the exam, you must get all the way up to the end. That doesn't mean you must answer everything; it just means the question is at the end and you'll need to enter and leave each section without answering the questions to void. There will be a question whether you want your exam voided or not. If you don't answer it, the timer will run out after five minutes, and your exam will be scored.

If you're even asking yourself the question whether you should or shouldn't void your exam, the answer is no, don't void your score.

Premeds are usually used to getting good grades and usually feeling pretty good about their performances on tests. The MCAT is a different beast. Most students walk out of it thinking they did terrible when, in reality, they likely did well. You can't let this subjective feeling lead you to void the exam.

If, on the other hand, you have a gut feeling that something just isn't right, like you feel you're taking a test in a foreign language and every question comes up and you're wondering when, not if you can void the MCAT, then you should probably void it.

What if I have a lot of blank answers?

It's okay to leave three or four questions blank. However, if you find that you've left two entire passages with about eleven or twelve questions blank, then this is an off day for you—think about voiding the test.

For most students who take full-length practice exams as we recommend—sitting for the full (almost) eight hours—they are usually well practiced enough that voiding the exam in the middle isn't an issue. It's usually the students who don't practice, who are in the middle of the MCAT, who start to freak out.

CHAPTER 7
LAST MINUTE MCAT TIPS

By the time test day rolls around, you'll feel like you've already spent an eternity studying for it. You may be overwhelmed, anxious, or even exhausted. You may be all three, but it is important that, at this point, you make rational decisions geared toward optimizing your performance on the exam.

While your impulse may be to try to continue cramming as much information as you can into your brain up until the last second, it will be more helpful to take a deep breath and plan a last-minute course of action that will allow you to destress as you complete your preparation. Instead of going berserk with science content, which will be counterproductive, use this time to take a measured approach toward practice testing and feeling your way through the experience of taking the real test.

An Outline of the Last Four Weeks

Four weeks before the exam

You'll want to take your first official AAMC scored practice exam roughly one month before your test date. The reason for this is that the AAMC exams are the best way to get the most accurate estimation of what you will score on the real MCAT. In addition, taking your first test this early will give you the necessary time to review your answers.

Unfortunately, the AAMC exams have a bad reputation for providing poor answer explanations. While the test itself is great, you'll probably find in reviewing your first AAMC scored tests that their explanations leave a lot to be desired.

This means you'll need to spend a good amount of time reviewing your scores and analyzing for yourself where exactly you went wrong. Part of the benefit of taking your first AAMC practice exam three weeks before the MCAT is that you'll have a few days during the week after to figure out the correct answers. During this time, it helps to pretend that the AAMC hired you to write answer explanations and commit to understanding the information necessary to do so. This will take time and commitment but will be the most efficient way of using your official practice exams.

If you have any other time left during that week, do some more timed practice. Your prep books and other resources will be full of questions; you'll want to spend time working your way through those.

If, at this point, you find that your score is nowhere near where it needs to be, now is the time to determine if you need to reschedule your MCAT test date. You don't want to miss the window of being able to reschedule and be forced to forfeit the money you paid for your exam.

Three weeks before the exam

Since the AAMC has released the third, scored full-length, you have an extra week of last-minute prep you can squeeze in. Three weeks before the MCAT, you'll do exactly what you did the week before, with the second AAMC full-length.

Two weeks before the exam

Use the second week before your exam to take the last AAMC scored practice test. Similar to the previous week, you want to use your test results to do a thorough analysis of your score and the reason you received it. While the AAMC, again, won't provide you with the best explanation answers, there are plenty of resources you can use to find the correct ones.

Assuming you took our advice and formed one, it is very helpful to use your study group during your final review period. Remember: these people are also preparing for the MCAT and are either having the same trouble you are or can help you with the answers you're not wrapping your head around. Utilizing your study group is going to be one of the most important aspects of your prep process in general, but it will be especially helpful when you're having difficulty with certain aspects of the MCAT practice tests.

One week before the exam

During the final week before your exam, you'll want to take the AAMC's unscored sample test. While this test is designed to help you prepare for the actual MCAT during your final week, it is not going to give you a score and will hopefully avoid adding unnecessary stress to your preparation.

The unscored sample test is different from the scored versions you've already taken in the sense that it does not translate to a scaled score. Many students have tried to estimate how they can quantify their sample test scores, but you should avoid doing this—it's not worth the stress. The scaled scores are only reliable with a lot of data, which the AAMC doesn't provide for the unsecured exam.

Instead, use the unscored test to simulate the process of taking the exam; prepare yourself for sitting through an eight-hour test day, and do the best you can.

Last-minute content review

While you study during the final week before your test, remind yourself that you cannot possibly review everything. Trying to do so will be entirely counter-productive. This isn't the point in the preparation process where you want to try to cram everything into your brain.

Instead, choose three things that consistently gave you trouble during your practice tests. Spend the week reviewing those topics and building your confidence to help ensure you can approach them assuredly during the MCAT.

Final day before your test

Of course, the day before your MCAT could be the most stressful time aside from the morning of the exam itself. While many students are so focused on the exam that they cannot imagine slowing down for the final day of preparation, you want to allow yourself to do as little prep work as possible. If you can avoid looking at prep materials and answering practice questions, you should. If you find yourself itching to continue studying for the MCAT, do so by simply reviewing your notes in a low-stress manner.

At this point, you want to think of yourself as a marathon runner. Runners and other athletes, after all, do a "taper" right before their race or competition. They've trained for months up to that day and make a point of not doing any physical activity the day before they compete. You're like an athlete in this situation, and your performance will benefit from a rest the same way theirs do.

Food

An often overlooked piece of the preparation for the MCAT test day is what you will eat. There are breaks that you should utilize to the best of your ability. Remember that the full break time includes checking in and checking out.

When you are taking your practice exams, try to eat what you are planning to eat during the actual test day. Do the same thing with your water intake. Because you aren't allowed to bring in any beverages, don't sip on anything while taking your practice full-lengths. Let your body discover what it's like to focus and crave something at the same time.

Maintaining good habits during the final weeks

Don't forget that during the final weeks of preparation, it is very important for you to keep a good sleep schedule, maintain your dietary habits, and get plenty of exercise. Additionally, make sure that you're drinking plenty of water, as hydration has a large impact on your cognition.

Remember that your brain is an organ just like the rest of them, and treating your body right with a proper diet, sleep and exercise will affect your brain positively.

At the same time, don't do anything that disrupts your body's normal homeostasis. Making large changes to your habits and diet during the days and weeks before the exam will not have a positive impact on your body.

At the end of the day, as you head toward your MCAT date, the biggest strength you have is your confidence. You have to trust that (hopefully after taking the advice in this book) you have done everything possible to prepare to the best of your ability for your MCAT test day. Believe in yourself and go crush it!

CHAPTER 8
WHAT THE TEST DAY WILL LOOK LIKE

As your MCAT preparation comes to a close (hopefully!) and you begin to get ready for the actual exam, you'll want to familiarize yourself with what exactly will happen when you show up at the testing location on your test day. Because you've prepared so heavily and invested so much time in test preparation, the exam day experience can be a stressful one. However, if you know the basic mechanics of what to expect, what you'll be asked to do, and how it all works, you'll be more equipped to handle the stress brought on by such a big day.

Check-In Process

Prior to test day, you'll get a number of notifications from the AAMC telling you to make sure the name appearing on your ID is the exact same name you used to register for the test. They do this because identification is taken very seriously on test day. Before you show up to take the MCAT, it is imperative that you double-check to make sure these names are identical and spelled the same way.

Once you provide identification at the check-in station, you'll receive a one-page, laminated sheet of rules and instructions. These are broad and obvious rules concerning theft, safety, and other things. After you've read the rules, you'll receive a locker key labeled with an assigned locker number. This is where you'll store your lunch, jacket and any other belongings you brought along with you. If you decide to keep your jacket or sweater on, you likely won't be able to take it off during the exam.

You want to make sure you leave your cell phone at home or in your car. While you are allowed to keep it in your locker, they will come get you and make you turn the phone off if it rings during the test. You'll lose valuable time by going through this process, so it is better to keep it somewhere that eliminates this risk. The only things you should have on you are your driver's license (or ID) and your locker key.

Before the test, you'll sit in the waiting room along with other test-takers for fifteen to twenty-five minutes depending on the location. If you get there early or it's a small testing center that's having a slow day, they may let you in earlier. This part will probably be boring and anxiety-inducing. Testing centers administer other tests, so not everyone there may be taking the MCAT.

At some point, though, they'll call your name, and you'll be led to a small room in between the waiting and testing rooms. This is where the security check takes place. You'll be asked to empty your pockets, your fingerprints will be scanned, or your palm will be scanned for your unique vein pattern, and you'll have your picture take. Then, you'll sign your name and list the testing time. From here, a proctor will lead you to your assigned cubicle.

When you sit down, a testing screen will be on the monitor in front of you with your picture to confirm your identity. Here, you'll confirm your name, and the program will run a tutorial on how to take the exam. Don't skip the tutorial. While the information is broad and repetitive, the tutorial is a good opportunity to get yourself settled in the cubicle. Take a minute to get a feel for the space and relax. There will be a keyboard at the testing station, but you won't use it at all during the test, so feel free to move it out of the way if that makes you more comfortable. Once the tutorial is over, the test will begin. It will look and feel just like all of your practice tests, assuming you did them with reputable companies.

What Can You Bring In to the Test?

During the check-in process listed above, you will need to put everything into the locker assigned to you. This means everything. There shouldn't be anything in your pants pockets. There shouldn't be anything in your jacket pockets. Any pockets on your person should be empty. They will be checked prior to going into the room.

The only things you are allowed to bring into the testing center are the wet-erase marker and laminated booklet the proctor gives you. If you wear glasses, you can wear those as well. You cannot bring in snacks or water to the testing room.

Gum Chewing

A common question from students is whether or not you're allowed to chew gum during the test. Since the exam (as of this writing) recently switched to Pearson as the testing center, their rules specifically say you are not allowed to chew gum. This may be a major change from the previous testing center, Prometric. If you search online, many students have previously said they were allowed to chew gum as long as they didn't disturb their neighbors.

How should I use my breaks and lunchtime?

Although you may be pumped up and jittery when it comes to break time, make sure that you take advantage of the time you have. You'll need to go through the checkout process where your fingerprints are scanned, and you'll put your signature on the sign-in sheet. Your breaks are ten minutes each, and lunch is thirty minutes. Those times include the check-out and check-in process.

You should use this time to move your body and get your blood flowing again. Your brain will benefit from moving your body around a bit. Do some jumping jacks or pace up and down the hall to refresh your brain. Additionally, make sure to grab a mouthful of food and some water while you have the chance. During lunch, have some sandwiches, granola bars or something else on hand that you can consume quickly. Try to eat as normal as possible during your lunch. If you haven't had a peanut butter and jelly sandwich since middle school, now is not the time to try it again.

Use the bathroom (even if you don't have to) to avoid having to go during the next section of the exam. While you're in the bathroom, you can take advantage of the opportunity to splash some water on your face and refresh yourself before heading back in to take the test. Don't forget to wash your hands!

Remember that thing we talked about previously – confidence? It comes in handy on test day! Be confident that you prepared. Don't second guess yourself as you are going through the exam. Don't get down on yourself during your breaks. You prepared well up to this point—trust yourself!

CHAPTER 9
MCAT STRATEGIES TO INCREASE YOUR SCORE

Using the booklet to your advantage

While you aren't allowed to bring any personal items into the testing area, the testing center will provide you with a nine-page booklet of laminated paper and wet-erase marker to use in whatever manner you find most helpful. These tools, while rudimentary, can really help you save time and move through the test more efficiently.

Essentially, there are three ways that you can use the booklet. The first approach would be not using it at all. This isn't necessarily the recommended approach, but it may be the best option for you if you find you're easily distracted or just won't benefit from the process of note-taking.

The second approach is to utilize the booklet for the purpose of summarizing. For example, you may find it helpful to summarize each paragraph as you read through the passages in each section of the exam. This can be helpful on both the science and verbal portions of the MCAT. This also, however, is not the most recommended approach to using the booklet, as you may end up spending valuable time writing and structuring your summaries instead of working on the questions. If you're not 100% positive that you need summaries to help you answer your questions, don't waste your time with this method. However, if you know yourself well enough to know that you need to summarize the information to process each question, this method may work from you.

It is important to remind yourself that wasted time can hurt your performance and that booklet should only be used in a way that doesn't detract from the rest of your test-taking process. For this reason, you may find that the best approach for you is to save the booklet only for those times when you really need it. If, for example, you bump into some passages or problems that you have trouble understanding or following the logic of, the booklet may be the perfect tool to help you better understand what the text is saying or asking. It may help, in this sense, to think of the booklet as a place where you can "think with your pencil." You can sort through jargon, map out the relationships between terms, and essentially use the booklet as a flow chart while you attempt to work out your answer to a particularly difficult problem.

Ultimately, use the booklet in a way that is most beneficial to your testing style. Like all other aspects of the test, you'll want to make sure you practice ahead of time and get familiar with the role the booklet plays in your MCAT testing experience. You can buy a laminated booklet like you'll see on your test day on Amazon and bring that or just bring paper and pencils to the library with you during your practice exams and pay attention to how you use them. Trying out different methods for using the booklet will prepare you to use them most efficiently when it comes time to take the real test.

Speed reading

One of the problems you may encounter while taking the MCAT is not having enough time to complete the test. This can be extremely frustrating. There is a popular myth that the MCAT is purposely designed to prevent you from completing the entire thing. This simply isn't true. It is true, however, that the test is designed to reward savvy test takers with strong time management skills and strategic tactics for thinking through problems. If you aren't strategically focused and tend to get lost in the details, you may find yourself running out of time on the exam.

This obviously doesn't mean you're a bad student. After all, as people engaged in science, we tend to be slow readers. Our education teaches us to read carefully and to absorb every detail before attempting to answer a problem. Unfortunately, the MCAT is not really about details. Instead, the test is much more about the main ideas of each passage. Therefore, doing well on the MCAT requires you to remember that you're looking for the big picture ideas, as opposed to minute details, of each passage on the exam. To get through all of the questions on the test, you'll have to read swiftly while simultaneously analyzing the information the passage is providing.

For most people, this is not a problem. The average reading speed for a college-educated adult is somewhere in the range of 200-400 words per minute. Even on the lower end, this means it will take around three minutes to read an average-sized MCAT passage. If, however, you find your reading speed is lower than 200 words per minute, you may want to find a reading technique course to help you prepare for the exam.

In order to diagnose your reading speed, time yourself reading a 300-400 word passage. You can do this the old-fashioned way (with a stopwatch/timer) or download any of the speed reading apps like Flash Reader, Accelerator, or Spreeder. You should be able to read and understand a 400-word passage in three to four minutes. If you find that you're taking six minutes or more to get an idea of what the passage is saying, you'll want to add a reading technique course to your preparation schedule.

Breaking down the answers

One of the most common mistakes that students make in approaching the MCAT is getting too wrapped up in the answer choices and details of each passage. Doing so can lead you to completely misunderstand what the question is asking in the first place.

To avoid this, you want to make sure you not only read the passage carefully but approach the questions themselves with an equal amount of attention. Stopping for just a second to carefully read and comprehend each question will vastly improve your chances of finding the correct answer.

When attempting to find the solution to each problem, then, it helps to get yourself into a rhythm of reading and understanding what the question is asking before attempting to solve the problem. After working through the passage, look at the question and determine what it wants from you. What does it expect you to do? Does it want you to solve a problem or does it want you to find information in the passage?

You will find it helpful to rephrase the question in your own words. If you can repeat the question back to yourself in different terms, you'll have a better idea of how you should be trying to answer it. From there, you'll be able to move forward with the necessary research.

In terms of choosing the right answer, there are two different techniques you may want to use. You might prefer to avoid looking at the answer choices and opt to predict the answer in advance, or you might choose to work through the process of elimination. Neither of these methods is inherently better or worse; there are pros and cons to each technique. Because each MCAT question often includes one or two "extreme" answers, you might find that using the process of elimination is an easy way for you to narrow down the potential correct answers. Whichever method you choose to find the right answer, it is important to remember that returning to the question is the best way to remind yourself what you're trying to accomplish.

Never leave a blank answer

After you're done breaking down the questions and answers, you may still not know the best answer. The one thing that you cannot do is leave an answer blank. If you read the beginning chapters on how the MCAT is scored, you'll remember that your score is based on the number of right answers you had. You are not marked off for wrong answers. Knowing this, you have no incentive for leaving an answer blank and nothing to lose for guessing. Using the skills above, try to narrow down the answers as much as possible and then make as much of an educated guess as you can before moving on to the next question.

Before you finish a section, make sure that every question has an answer. If you are coming down to the last few minutes, go back and fill in as many answers as you can before time runs out.

Using flashcards

Flashcards are one of the most popular study tools available. They can be a great way to build repetition into your study process and drill content into your brain that might otherwise be difficult to remember. For this reason, flashcards are recommended to any student preparing to take the MCAT.

There are a variety of different types of flashcards available on the market. The AAMC's flashcard deck, for example, provides you with 100 discrete questions, printed with the question on one side and the answer on the other. This is the most common format of flashcard and works well for most people; this is also a format that you can duplicate on your own. Instead of purchasing a deck of 100 cards, it might make more sense for you to create your own flashcards. Doing so will give you the opportunity to study and learn new material as you work through the process of transcribing questions and answers onto the cards. While the benefit of buying a deck from the AAMC is that the questions are coming from the expert source, Q Books and study guides usually contain much more than 100 questions. Therefore, comparatively small decks of flashcards do not provide the most value for your money.

At the same time, you may find that physical flashcards are not even the best way for you to study. If you're not an old-fashioned studier, then digital flashcards might be the best route for you to take. There are a ton of apps out there specifically designed to help students study for tests. Brainscape, for example, is a great app for those preparing for the MCAT. This app allows you to rate each flashcard on a scale of one to five, depending on how difficult it was for you. It then recycles each card back into the deck and shows you the cards you found difficult more frequently than those you found easier. Using Brainscape, you'll have the ability to customize your flashcard study process and work toward mastering the content you need to work on the most.

Similarly, Anki is an app that allows you to study with flashcards using your mobile device. Unlike Brainscape, Anki doesn't provide you with prewritten questions but does allow you to upload your own cards to the platform. The nice thing about Anki is that it contains a database of user-submitted card sets that you can use to study. While you want to be careful about the cards you choose (as you can't be sure who submitted them), this can be a great app for studying digitally.

Whichever approach you take to studying with flashcards, remember that it's never too early to start. If you're thinking about medical school in a serious way, flashcards can be a great tool to start using as early as your freshman year. The repetitive nature of flashcards can provide a learning technique that allows you to hold onto that precious undergraduate course material, ensuring that it's still in your head when it comes time for you to take the MCAT.

How to make the most of mnemonics

If you're like most people, you may believe that mnemonics are all about making a sentence with the first letter of everything you're trying to memorize. Children are taught "ROY G BIV," for example, to remember the colors of the spectrum (Red, Orange, Yellow, Green, Blue, Indigo, and Violet). However, these aren't the only kinds of mnemonic devices. While you can develop these kinds of mnemonic devices to help you remember scientific information, this isn't where mnemonics end. The truth is that mnemonics can be used to help you remember things through auditory, visual and kinesthetic means.

Auditory mnemonics are the ones with which we are most familiar. They usually take the form of acronyms you can say out loud which will remind you of the thing you need to remember. "ROY G BIV" is an example of an auditory mnemonic device. A good science example is "Have No Fear Of Ice Cold Beer," a mnemonic device designed to help you remember the diatomic gasses (Hydrogen, Nitrogen, Fluorine, Oxygen, Iodine, Chlorine, Bromine). All good auditory mnemonics are catchy and will pop into your head when prompted.

Other forms of auditory mnemonics include narrative stories and songs. If it helps you to remember information in the form of a catchy tune, try making one up until it sticks in your brain. Alternatively, if stories about the information help you to recall it later, then look for narratives around the topic to help you remember it.

At the same time, you may be a more visually-oriented person and might prefer visual mnemonics to auditory ones. Instead of using "Have No Fear Of Ice Cold Beer" to remember the diatomic gasses, you could remember them by implanting in your memory the fact that these gasses make a kind of L-shape on the periodic table. If you're a visual learner, you'll benefit from mnemonic devices that require visual engagement rather than auditory memory.

You also have the option of using kinesthetic mnemonic devices, which help you to recall information through physical and spatial means. For example, when thinking about magnetic fields, think of your thumb as hitchhiking along with the current. Your fingers are the magnetic field. Your palm pushing is the force vector coming out at a right angle from your hand. Hold your hand in front of you and connect those ideas kinesthetically to the way your hands move around. For some folks, being able to use physical reality as a way to remember important information will be very helpful.

Whichever type of mnemonics you decide to use, make sure that they are personal and memorable. This will increase the likelihood that you'll be able to remember them when you need to. Sometimes, the more outrageous they are, the better they work.

However, make sure that you never use mnemonics as a first plan of attack. If you're a good science student, you probably already have a strong memory and mnemonics should only be used to remember those things which you otherwise have a very difficult time memorizing. Ideally, mnemonics are used to fit things in your brain when you just can't get them to fit in any other way.

CHAPTER 10
HOW DOES THE MCAT AFFECT ADMISSION TO MEDICAL SCHOOL

Medical school admissions is a rough job. Each Admissions Committee is looking to put together the best class of students for their institution every year. The MCAT usually plays a big part in how they evaluate your application to determine if you will be a good student or not. In this chapter, we'll cover the various aspects of the MCAT and how each may affect your chances of getting an interview and ultimately getting accepted into medical school.

What is a competitive MCAT score?

For students who have grown used to getting straight A's and perfect scores throughout their academic career, the MCAT scoring system can be somewhat frustrating. After all, the likelihood of getting a perfect 100% is very slim and understanding whether you got a good score is slightly more subjective than a 0-100 grading scale. As opposed to thinking of your score in terms of letter grades, it helps to assess scores by whether they'll help you get into the school in which you want to enroll.

Whereas in schools an F is objectively bad and an A+ is objectively good, when taking the MCAT a "good" score is any score that will benefit your application. This will, obviously, be a different score depending on who you are and what your goal is. You want to have a score that places you among the average students who are accepted into a given school, if not higher. That's not to say you won't get in with a lower score. This is just to help you shoot for a target.

Out of all MCAT test takers, the average score is around a 500. This is the midpoint on the MCAT's scoring range of 472 to 528 and the median score received by the most number of applicants who take the test each year. However, in the 2016-2017 application cycle, only 39% of all applicants were accepted into schools[6], which shows that getting an average score will not necessarily help you get into medical school. While plenty of applicants who receive scores of 501 or 502 do get interviews and acceptances every year, to be competitive, you need to shoot higher than just getting the national average.

We recommend that you aim to receive a score of 508 or higher. This will place you within the 80th percentile of applicants who take the MCAT each year and in line with the majority of those 39% of people accepted to schools. According to the 2016-2017 AAMC data, the mean MCAT score for matriculants was 508.7.

Remember, your MCAT score is not the sole component of your application and will be considered in relation to the rest of your application. This means that a good score can only help your application and a bad score can only hurt it. Scoring a 508, while placing you among the average accepted student, is still no guarantee that you'll get an acceptance or even an interview. We can't stress it enough that the MCAT is just one part of your application. Scoring a 510, or higher, on the MCAT can only benefit your overall application (unless you're only applying to schools like Harvard, Stanford, and Wash U., in which case you'll want to aim as high as humanly possible).

If you look at table 23 from the AAMC[7], you'll notice that more than 10% of students with an MCAT score higher than 517 and a

GPA greater than 3.79 were not accepted into medical school during the 2016-2017 cycle. While this may be surprising, it reflects the fact that your test scores and grades are not the only things you'll be assessed on when applying to medical school. These applicants, while scoring higher and performing better in school than most other people, were not accepted due to another factor in the application process. It may have been a poor interview, a weak personal statement or a lack of strong recommendations. For whatever reason, their scores were not competitive enough to get them accepted.

This should be a reminder, then, that a competitive score is only relative to the rest of your application's circumstances. Even those who score well above average still have to consider their MCAT score in relation to other things.

You'll have to assess your own application and decide which scores are going to be competitive at the schools you want to attend. To figure out what you want to receive on the test, research the requirements or average scores at your school of choice and consider your application's strengths and weaknesses. In the end, a competitive score is one that pairs well enough with your personal statement, interview, GPA, life experience, and recommendations to get you in the door of your chosen school.

Does it hurt to take it more than once?

It seems to be a common question, but there is no definitive answer as to whether taking the MCAT more than once will be detrimental to your chances of getting into a medical school. This depends on the admissions process of the schools to which you're applying. In some cases, schools will place the greatest emphasis on your most recent score, which means that retaking the exam would help you only if your scores improve with each test. In other cases, however, the highest score might be used when looking at your application, no matter which test you received it on.

Sometimes, medical schools will gauge your MCAT testing ability by using the average of any test scores you received. Again, this means that retaking the test won't harm your application as long as there is an increase in scores with each test.

The reality of the situation is that most students who retake the test earn scores that are either exactly the same or two points different from their previous score. Their scores don't really change much. If you need a big boost in your scores, you might need to think through the process even more.

Ultimately, for your retakes to be worth the time and money you'll spend on them, you'll want to make sure that you're scoring better than your previous test by more than just a point or two. Remember, while scoring the same or lower may not always hurt you, getting a better score on your second or third time taking the test can only help your application. Alongside this, remind yourself that you'll only get a better score if your study process is more calculated and rigorous each time you take the exam. If you do decide to retake the MCAT, make sure you are analyzing your weaknesses and developing study habits which will help you to achieve the score you want.

Is there a best time to take the MCAT for admission purposes?

While the MCAT testing season is long and there are numerous options as to when you can take it, you should make sure to take the exam at the point when it best fits into your application schedule. This means that, because medical school applications open in the late spring, you should take the MCAT early enough so you can decide whether to retake it if you are unhappy with your scores.

One of the biggest things students aren't aware of when it comes to medical school admissions is that most medical schools accept students on a rolling admissions basis. This means that the earlier your application is complete, including having your MCAT scores, the sooner you may be invited for an interview, and the earlier in the cycle you can gain acceptance. The longer you wait, the more your chances of being accepted decrease, because medical schools are already filling up their classes and running out of interview spots.

When deciding on your MCAT test date, remember that it takes a month for your scores to be returned to you, so you'll have to account for this block of time when planning your application process. If you find out in August that your scores weren't up to par, for example, this will require you to prepare and test again, delaying your final MCAT scores to schools and further delaying your application. Doing so can leave you stressed out and will potentially result in you not receiving any interviews, even if you do well on your final attempt, so take the MCAT early enough to avoid this.

Will a great MCAT score help me if I have a low GPA?

There is a common thought that MCAT scores and GPAs are on opposite ends of a scale and that a great MCAT score will balance below average GPAs. This is a tricky one because GPAs come in all shapes and sizes. You may have had a poor start to your undergrad years but crushed your last couple years. You might be the opposite, having burned out and struggled to cross the finish line.

Let's assume that you're completely balanced every year and you have a cumulative GPA of 2.8 and a science GPA of 2.8. No MCAT score is going to help you. Your GPA is just not competitive enough. Only about 6% of the students with a 2.8 GPA get accepted into medical school[8]. What the table doesn't show you is that these students might have graduate degrees with great GPAs that help offset the 2.8 undergraduate GPA, giving the admissions committee more reassurance of the student's ability to do well in medical school.

What if you have a strong upward trend, meaning you struggled early, but have finally learned how you study best and are crushing your classes now? You have a 2.8 cumulative and science GPA but your last two years of school are close to a 4.0. Because your GPA is still below the arbitrary line of 3.0, you will have a harder time with your applications, no matter your MCAT score.

If you can show a great upward trend in your classes, especially in the sciences, a GPA above a 3.0, with a strong MCAT, it might just tip the scales for you. At the end of the day, your MCAT score and GPA are just two parts of the application, so you don't want to just focus on those aspects.

If my scores are unbalanced, will that hurt me?

Unbalanced scores occur when you perform vastly worse on one section of the test than on the others. This can be a red flag in your application and may prevent you from getting into the school you want to attend. Some applicants, for example, do very poorly on the CARS section of the test due to putting too much effort into studying for the sciences and being under the impression that their CARS scores aren't as important. However, many programs consider the CARS to be the most important part of the test and look for students who perform well on that section. Some Canadian medical schools are known to just look at the CARS score. These programs know that they have the resources to teach you everything you need to know about being a doctor, but want to make sure you come into their program with the ability to communicate verbally and on paper.

If you perform very poorly (less than 123) on the CARS or any other section of the test, you'll most likely want to consider doing a retake. However, whether a low score on any given section will hurt your application ultimately depends on what your exact scores are and the schools to which you're applying. Some schools will filter out all applicants that have lower than a 125 on any given section of the exam. Although your application will be reviewed holistically, taking into consideration every component of your test scores, academic profile, career history and life experience, medical schools often create streamlined processes for sorting through the initial applications. If you have extremely low scores on one section of the exam, you run the risk of being filtered out simply based on the rubric the school is using to find the students they want to accept.

At the same time, many schools will accept students with low CARS scores. Always remember that whether you need to retake the MCAT is contingent on your circumstances and is a decision you'll have to make through an assessment of yourself in relation to the school to which you're applying. There is no standard response to unbalanced scores. To determine if you should retake the test, try contacting the admissions committee at the school to which you're applying. They may be able to look at your situation and let you know whether you should schedule a retake.

Should I wait to submit my applications until I have my MCAT score?

While you can apply to medical school without having taken your MCAT, most medical schools will not review your application until they have received your scores. For this reason, applying to school without having gone through the exam or received your scores will present a few risks.

If you do poorly on the MCAT but have already applied to school, you risk putting yourself in the position of having to rely on those scores or retake the test, further delaying when your application will be complete. In the case that you took the MCAT early enough, around May, and received your score just after submitting, retaking the exam may not be as big of a problem. The biggest issue comes from students who rush a retake, to "save" an application, and they don't properly analyze why they didn't do well in the first place, repeating the same mistakes on their retake. This results in another poor score, often lower than the first due to increased stress and self-imposed pressure.

You may read all of that and think we're advocating for not applying until you get your scores. Actually, we're not. You should apply to school as early in the application cycle as possible. You want your transcripts verified early; the longer you wait to apply, the longer it takes to get verified. There is a balance though. You don't want applications to get in the way of studying for the MCAT either. When secondaries arrive, after your application has been verified and transmitted to schools, you want to turn those around as soon as possible. MCAT prep might get in the way of that.

At the end of the day, you need to take the MCAT when you are ready, and you need to balance that with a strong, early application to medical school. If for some reason, you need to take the MCAT later in the cycle, you may want to hold off on applying for another year.

CHAPTER 11
YOUR NEXT STEP TO PREPARE FOR THE MCAT

The best preparation includes a mix of content review, passage practice, and full-length exams. However you prepare, the core is a good strategy for tackling passages and then plenty of practice to solidify that strategy.

While some books will offer only a single strategy, real prep involves trying out a number of different approaches and finding the method that works best for you. Every student is unique, and good prep should build on your unique strengths and weaknesses. In the two chapters that follow, we have included the introductory strategy chapters taken from Next Step Test Preparation's Strategy & Practice books for the Biology and Biochemistry and the Critical Analysis and Reasoning Skills sections of the MCAT. The strategies presented in the Biology and Biochemistry section that follows are applicable to all three science sections on the exam, and the general reasoning and analysis skills presented in the CARS chapter are applicable to the entire exam.

If you would like additional practice applying these strategies, consider purchasing additional Next Step Test Prep MCAT books, or signing up for a free online bundle including a free full-length practice MCAT, a free diagnostic test, a free science content diagnostic as well as other free resources. You can do so at: mcatbook.com/freetest.

1 https://en.wikipedia.org/wiki/Medical_College_Admission_Test

2 https://www.aamc.org/download/321494/data/factstablea16.pdf

3 https://jamanetwork.com/journals/jama/fullarticle/2319163

4
https://www.aamc.org/download/473038/data/overview2016testingyear_res
ources.pdf

5 https://aamc-
orange.global.ssl.fastly.net/production/media/filer_public/d8/a4/d8a4f75f-
99a8-4303-a828-5564cbc3e810/retestertotalscorechange.pdf

6 https://www.aamc.org/download/321494/data/factstablea16.pdf

7 https://www.aamc.org/download/321508/data/factstablea23.pdf

8 https://www.aamc.org/download/321508/data/factstablea23.pdf

SECTION II
STRATEGY AND PRACTICE

CHAPTER 12
SCIENCE SECTIONS PASSAGES AND QUESTION STRATEGIES

Independent Questions

The Bio/Biochem section can be difficult for many students. These sciences may be more familiar to many premeds than the physical science content but there's also so much material to learn. As we wrote earlier in this book, the difficulty of the test is in how it tests the material, not necessarily *what* material it tests. However, a focused strategy can help you score more points through understanding the material on a fundamental level, as opposed to superficial memorizing.

As we mentioned in the Introduction, each Bio/Biochem Section will consist of 15 independent questions and 44 passage-based questions. Time is tight on the MCAT and you'll want to make sure you make the most of each minute.

To that end, the first thing you should do when you start the timer is go through the section and complete all of the independent questions. They're typically arranged in clumps of three to four questions and will say something like **"The following questions are not based on a descriptive passage."** at the top of the screen.

To start, we'll look at a few examples of these sorts of independent questions.

1. A patient with a tumor in his hypothalamus experiences a significant increase in vasopressin secretion from his posterior pituitary. Which of the following would be the most direct consequence of this disorder?

   A) Increased water concentration in the urine

B) Increased total urine volume

C) Decreased sodium ion concentration in plasma

D) Increased secretion of thyroxine

This is an example of a relatively straightforward biology question. When reading through these independent questions, start by asking yourself, *"Exactly what is the question asking me for?"*. A classic sort of trap answer will be something that's the "right answer to the wrong question" - that is, it will be related to the topic of the question and will be a true fact, but not *exactly* answer the question.

Here, the question is asking us what the function of vasopressin is, though in a roundabout way. Once you've read the question and answer choices, and you know *exactly* what the question is asking for, ask yourself, *"What information is provided?"*. You've got to be careful not to make any unwarranted assumptions. The MCAT is a picky test and will expect you to pay attention to the exact information provided. We're told that the patient in question has a tumor that leads to *over-expression* of vasopressin and asks you for a likely consequence of the increased hormone level.

Next, ask yourself, *"What outside information do I need?"*. The independent questions especially will draw heavily on outside knowledge. Here, you need to be familiar with the physiological function of vasopressin. Vasopressin, also known as antidiuretic hormone, is a peptide hormone found in humans and other mammals. Its two primary functions are to retain water in the body and to constrict blood vessels. Vasopressin regulates the body's osmolarity by acting to increase water reabsorption in the collecting ducts of the kidney nephron. This results in more concentrated urine and more water present in the plasma. The increase in water in the plasma would decrease the concentration of sodium ions in the body.

Finally, *evaluate the choices, either by prediction or process of elimination*. In "prediction" you simply skim quickly through the choices looking for what you already know the answer will say. That's often the case when you have a good content background in an area. If you're not exactly sure what they're looking for, don't delay – start eliminating choices.

Remember, **answer every question, even if you're not sure!**

In this question, the answer is (C). Decreased sodium ion concentration in plasma. By its regulation of plasma osmolarity, the excess vasopressin in this patient will cause the patient to develop more concentrated urine and more water present in the plasma. The increase in water in the plasma would decrease the concentration of sodium ions in the body. Thus, the correct answer is (C).

A: This is the opposite of vasopressin's effect. A greater degree of water reabsorption would lower the levels of water in the urine, thus decreasing the concentration of water in the fluid excreted.

B: This is the opposite of the effects of vasopressin. Greater water retention by the kidney would serve to lower total urine volume, not increase it. This could be result of a tumor that *lowers* vasopressin release, which is why it is important to be sure of exactly what the question is asking.

D: This answer is another MCAT favorite, the one that comes out of left field, but may seem plausible if you're unsure of your content. Vasopressin is a hormone that exerts homeostatic regulation via its effects on the kidney, which is not directly involved in the actions of the thyroid, which maintains homeostasis of the body via temperature control. The thyroid controls metabolism through the effects of the thyroid hormone, thyroxine, which acts to raise metabolic activity in the body. Thus vasopressin is not directly linked to metabolic rate, which thyroxine controls.

Now try another similar question:

2. Which of the following is an example of disruptive selection?

A) Females of a species choose to mate with males of the species based on the size and color of the males' tail feathers, with females preferentially mating with males that have larger and more colorful plumage.

B) An insect is preyed upon by several different species of bird that rely on vision for hunting, such that the birds are more easily able to see, catch, and eat the larger insects.

C) A type of trout competes with another fish species for food and in such competition, trout that are significantly larger than average are able to intimidate the other fish species away and trout that are significantly smaller than average are able to access food by stealth without confrontation.

D) In a certain species of crocodile, females that are smaller than average are subject to predation by snakes and females that are larger than average are subject to hunting by humans.

Exactly what is the question asking me for?

A situation that provides a clear example of the concept of disruptive selection.

What information is provided?

You have been given the name of the genetic concept to which you must match the answer, disruptive selection.

What outside knowledge do I need?

The MCAT will expect you to be familiar with the various theories and concepts in the biological sciences and to recognize them when shown an unfamiliar scenario.

Disruptive selection is a form of natural selection pressure in which members of a species gain an advantage by not being of the average type. Here, choice C gives us an example where especially large and especially small fish have a competitive advantage. This "disrupts" the population by leading to smaller and smaller fish and also larger and larger fish. Eventually these two types of fish may develop into entirely separate species.

A: This is an example of sexual selection, a mode of natural selection in which some individuals out-reproduce other member of a population because they are better at securing mates.

B: This is an example of directional selection, with smaller insects being favored. Directional selection is a mode of natural selection in which the environmental conditions favor an extreme phenotype over other phenotypes, causing the allele frequency to shift over time in the direction of the extreme phenotype.

D: This is an example of stabilizing selection. Stabilizing selection is a type of natural selection that favors the average individuals in a population. This process selects against the extreme phenotypes and instead favors the majority of the population that is well adapted to the environment, with average member of the species being favored.

Now that we've carefully examined a couple of questions, complete the questions on the next page to practice this process. The explanations follow.

3. When exposed to milk contaminated with strontium, children's bodies will incorporate the strontium into their bones. The strontium tends to locate primarily in growing long bones. If examined, where would strontium most likely be found?
A) Along the outer edges of the ala of the hips
B) Near the sutures in skull bones
C) Evenly distributed along the tibias
D) The epiphyseal plates of the femurs

4. At the end of an organic chemistry reaction a student is left with the end product in a 100mL aqueous solution. She attempts to do an extraction using 25mL of acetone. Which of the following correctly characterizes the results she will see?
A) The extraction will work given acetone's relative solubility in water.
B) The extraction would work with acetone or any other organic solvent since organic molecules are insoluble in water.
C) The student should instead perform a distillation, as distillation is the only method that can separate an organic solute from an aqueous solvent.
D) The extraction will be unsuccessful since acetone is miscible in water.

5. Following a stroke, a patient loses certain motor functions leaving him unable to write with a pen. After months of rehab he slowly

regains this ability. This demonstrates:

A) the regrowth of damaged tissues.

B) neural plasticity.

C) central nervous system functions being taken over by the peripheral nervous system.

D) the substitution of regrown glial cell function for neuronal cell function.

6. A soldier is exposed to a nerve gas which, when inhaled, binds irreversibly and non-competitively to acetylcholinesterase. The soldier is mostly likely to die from:

A) tetanic contraction of the diaphragm.

B) hypovolemic shock.

C) gangrene.

D) stroke.

Independent Question Explanations

3. When exposed to milk contaminated with strontium, children's bodies will incorporate the strontium into their bones. The strontium tends to locate primarily in growing long bones. If examined, where would strontium most likely be found?

A) Along the outer edges of the ala of the hips.

B) Near the sutures in skull bones.

C) Evenly distributed along the tibias.

D) The epiphyseal plates of the femurs.

The question states that strontium localizes to the growing portion of long bones, and long bones grow along their epiphyseal plates. There are four bone shapes in the human skeleton – long bones, short bones, flat bones, and irregular bones. Long bones have a tubular shaft and articular surface at each end (e.g the bones of the arms and legs). Short bones have a tubular shaft and articular surfaces at each end but are much smaller compared to the long bones. The short bones include all of the small bones in the hands, the feet, and the clavicle. Flat bones are thin and have broad surfaces. The flat bones include the scapula, the ribs, and the sternum. Irregular bones are irregular in size and shape. They include the bones in the vertebral column, the carpal bones in the hands, tarsal bones in the feet, and the patella. The hips and the skull are flat bones, not long bones, so you may eliminate choices A and B. The question states that strontium localizes to the growing portion of long bones, and long bones grow along their epiphyseal plates. Thus choice D is correct.

A: The ilium (ala) is the uppermost and largest bone of the pelvis, and is a flat bone.

B: The skull and cranial bones are flat bones, not long bones.

C: Very tempting, because is does mention a long bone, the tibia, also known as the shin bone. However, the longitudinal growth of long bones is a result of ossification at the epiphyseal plate.

4. At the end of an organic chemistry reaction a student is left with the end product in a 100mL aqueous solution. She attempts to do an extraction using 25mL of acetone. Which of the following correctly characterizes the results she will see?

   A) The extraction will work given acetone's relative solubility in water.

   B) The extraction would work with acetone or any other organic solvent since organic molecules are insoluble in water.

   C) The student should instead perform a distillation, as distillation is the only method that can separate an organic solute from an aqueous solvent.

   D) The extraction will be unsuccessful since acetone is miscible in water.

   To carry out an extraction, the two liquids mixed must not be soluble in each other. They will separate out forming two layers in the test tube, and the solutes within them will spontaneously sort to the layer in which they are more soluble. Acetone, as a very polar molecule, readily dissolves in water. Thus it's impossible to do a water-acetone extraction and choice D is the correct answer.

A: This is the exact opposite of the right answer, as described above.

B: Many organic molecules are soluble in water, including acetone and many alcohols.

C: There are many methods by which solutes can be separated from their solvent, not just distillation.

5. Following a stroke, a patient loses certain motor functions leaving him unable to write with a pen. After months of rehab he slowly regains this ability. This demonstrates:

A) the regrowth of damaged tissues.

B) neural plasticity.

C) central nervous system functions being taken over by the peripheral nervous system.

D) the substitution of regrown glial cell function for neuronal cell function.

Although parts of the brain are specialized for certain functions, when the brain is damaged some of that function can return through neural plasticity. The brain uses a new part to carry out the old function.

A: The central nervous system does not regrow neurons.

C: The peripheral nervous system functions to transport signals to and from the CNS and does not carry out complicated tasks like writing with a pen.

D: The glia (e.g. Schwann cells and oligodendrocytes) are supporting cells and do not carry out nerve function themselves.

6. A soldier is exposed to a nerve gas which, when inhaled, binds irreversibly and non-competitively to acetylcholinesterase. The soldier is mostly likely to die from:

A) tetanic contraction of the diaphragm.

B) hypovolemic shock.

C) gangrene.

D) stroke.

Acetylcholinesterase is the enzyme in the neuromuscular junction that breaks down acetylcholine. This breakdown is necessary for a nerve to stop stimulating a muscle to contract – the enzyme allows the muscle to relax. If this poison gets to the diaphragm, it would not be allowed to relax, preventing the victim from exhaling. This would asphyxiate the person.

> B, D: Shock and stroke relate to problems with the circulatory system, rather than the neuromuscular system.

> C: Nothing in the question stem suggests the soldier would have infected tissue subject to gangrene, a potentially life-threatening condition that arises when a considerable mass of body tissue dies.

Bio/Biochem Science Passages

The science passages on the MCAT will be anywhere from 250-550 words, and will often come with one or more diagrams. The types of information they present can be broadly categorized as informational or experimental. There are a number of different approaches possible here, but in this book we will opt for a relatively simple one: use the on-screen highlighter.

Some folks may like to go slowly and use the booklet provided to take notes, and others prefer to skim very quickly through the passage to get to the questions as quickly as possible. For some students those might work. But at least at first, we suggest you start with our "middle of the road" approach: don't skip right to the questions, don't bother taking notes on the booklet. Instead, read briskly – a little faster than you're normally comfortable with – and highlight important ideas as they come up.

When you come to experimental information, slow down and focus on one question: **what did they measure?** The MCAT loves to test your understanding of a passage by focusing on exactly what the experiment measured.

So what should you highlight?

There are four general categories of things worth highlighting: **Key terms, opinions, contrasts, cause and effect relationships.**

Keep in mind, we're using these category names *very* loosely. What matters is that you've spotted a key idea, not what name you give it. Having said that, here's what to watch for:

Key terms: These are things like proper nouns, technical terms, numbers, dates, etc. They're the words that you're going to want to be able to find again quickly if a question asks about them.

Opinions: Most importantly, the author's. Opinions can be a view expressed by a particular scientist, or a view espoused by a school of thought. The main thing to watch for here is the emphasis words like *should, ought, must, better, worse,* etc. These are rare, but not absent in the science passages.

Contrast: Just what it says. Watch for conflicting views, old vs. new, traditional vs. radical and so on. In science passages contrasts typically show up as opposite functions or effects (e.g. glucagon vs. insulin).

Cause and effect: We're going to use the phrase "cause and effect" to refer to any logical connection, association, correlation, or literal cause and effect relationship presented in the passages. Any time the passages offers us a "because this, therefore that" relationship, we'll call it "cause and effect". To be clear, we don't mean these are always literal, scientific causes. Rather, we're using this phrase in a loose, rhetorical way.

Figures: When you are presented with a figure/table/graph on the MCAT, is it important to approach it as you do the text. Focus on identifying the main purpose to the figure. For example, what relationship, findings, results, or data does it present? What kind of information is it (numbers, graphs, a schematic). Once you have identified what type of information it presents and what implications it could have on the type of questions asked, move on. You do not need to decipher the entire graphic now, if it is important, the questions will ask about it and we can earn points.

While using this book, have a yellow highlighter marker handy. Highlight in the book just like you would want to on the real exam. When you review the explanations afterwards, you'll see that we break down the material a couple of ways.

First, we use **bold and <u>underline</u>** text to show you the words and phrases you should have highlighted. Then, underneath each paragraph, we use **bold text** to describe *why* you should highlight those terms. The material is analyzed using the four categories above.

If you're the type of test-taker who likes to take notes on the booklet, then our **bold text** notes under the paragraph can serve as an example of the sorts of things you should have jotted down. Recall that on test day, time is a factor so when note taking, shorthand and abbreviations are an ideal way to convey full sentences worth of information without needing to write in complete sentences.

Another valuable strategy for the MCAT is to prioritize your quicker, easier points while saving tougher passages for later. Thus, it is in your best interest to practice all relevant topics on the exam. This will allow you to identify areas of strength and areas of weakness. Once identified, weaker areas can be attacked with diligent practice.

Passage Format

In addition to using content, you can also utilize the type of passage and the category of figures presented to prioritize passages. The images will also allow you to quickly identify the passage content.

Before jumping into a passage, take a few seconds to **scan the passage** for any figures, graphs, and equations. Next try to **identify the topic of the passage**. This will allow you ask yourself several important questions before you begin reading.

1) *"How comfortable am I with the presented topic?"*
2) *"How well do I recognize the ideas presented in the figures?"*
3) *"Is the format of the passage one with which I am comfortable"*

The MCAT will present Bio/Biochem science passages in three different formats. In the Bio/Biochem section they are:

1) **Information based passages:** These passages will be dense on information about a topic, and may present equations or figures related to that topic. However, they will not be centered around a research principle or experimental procedure.

2) **Experiment based passages:** These passages will be built around a specific experimental procedure. The goal here will be to identify the goals, results and implications of the experiments performed. A solid understanding of what and why the experimenters carried out tasks is much more important to your reading than the exact details of the procedure.

3) **Research based passages:** These passages are a hybrid of the other two passage formats. They will present a core concept of Bio/Biochem (typically with a medical slant) but they will do so in the context of a research project. The research passages released so far are broader in their scientific focus than the experiment based passages. This also allows the MCAT to introduce questions that specifically test you on the design and execution of medically related research.

Question Format

Once you have completed the passage reading, it is on to the **questions**, which is **where all the points are!** Just like the passages, each question the exam presents is looking to test your ability to complete a task. The four question types are:

Task 1, Recall: 35% or about 20-21 questions.

Task 2, Problem Solving: 45% or about 26-27 questions.

Task 3, Research Design: 10% or about 5-6 questions.

Task 4, Data-Based and Statistical Reasoning: 10% or about 5-6 questions.

Task 1: Recall of Scientific Concepts

A big part of your success both in medical school and on the MCAT is demonstrating a solid understanding of scientific concepts and principles. The exam will test your ability to recall key formulas and concepts and your ability to identify the relationship between closely related concepts.

Task 1 Example Question

7. A patient undergoes a radiation treatment that destroys all of his bone marrow. Which of the following would be expected to remain at normal levels despite this treatment?
A) Erythrocytes
B) Platelets
C) Monocytes
D) None of the above

This is a task 1 question because it simply requires you to recall the function of the bone marrow. The bone marrow is responsible for making both red blood cells, choice A, as well as the cells involved in immune response, choice C, and in blood clotting, choice B. Thus destruction of the bone marrow would not allow any of these cell types to remain at normal levels and choice D is the correct answer.

Task 2: Problem Solving within Scientific Concepts

The MCAT is not just about recall. The exam tests a student's critical reasoning about scientific concepts, theories, and applications. Solving these questions will involve analyzing and assessing scientific explanations and predictions across chemistry and physics. You will see plenty of these questions in this book but take a look at the sample question below.

Task 2 Example Question

8. A woman who is a carrier for a sex-linked recessive trait marries a man whose father was affected by that trait. If they have a daughter, what is the probability that the daughter will be a carrier for the trait and the probability that she will have the trait, respectively?

   A) 0, 0
   B) ½, 0
   C) ½, ½
   D) 1, ½

   This is a task 2 question, and you must use knowledge from classical genetics to solve this problem. In addition to recalling the concept of sex-linked recessive traits, this is a task 2 question because it requires you to apply the scientific principle of the genetic crosses to determine the genotypes of hypothetical offspring. Building the Punnett square, a diagram that is used to predict an outcome of a particular cross or breeding experiment, will allow you to arrive at the conclusion that any generation 1 daughters cannot express the disease. The genotypes of the parents are X^cX and XY. The father does not have the trait. Sex-linked traits cannot be passed from father to son since fathers only pass the Y chromosome to sons. So the fact that the grandfather had the trait is irrelevant. We're explicitly told that the mother is a carrier so we know her genotype is X^cX.

	X	Y
X	XX	XY
X^c	X^cX	X^cY

Doing a cross we see that ½ the daughters will be genotype X^cX and ½ will be XX. So the odds of being a carrier are ½ and the odds of having the trait are 0. Thus choice B is correct.

Task 3: Research Design

The new MCAT is looking to identify well-rounded future physicians. It will ask you to display a clear understanding of crucial components of scientific research. These questions will test your scientific inquiry skills by showing that you can actually design can carry out the "business" of science. You will be tested on your mastery of important components of scientific methodology.

To answer these questions correctly you will need to understand the methods that social, natural, and behavioral scientists conduct research designed to test and expand the boundaries of science. These questions may seek to test your ability to recognize the ethical guidelines scientists must follow to ensure the rights of research subjects, the integrity of their work, and the interests of research sponsors.

Task 3 Example Question

9. The electrophoresis gel used in protein analysis contains SDS, a 12 member hydrocarbon chain attached to a sulfate group. Multiple SDS molecules will bind to the uncovered hydrophobic regions of denatured proteins. The use of SDS in electrophoresis works by allowing separation of proteins solely based on which property?

A) Quaternary structure
B) Tertiary structure
C) Water solubility

D) Molecular weight

This is a task 3 question and requires knowledge of protein structure as well as analytical lab techniques. To answer this question you must understand the design of a protein electrophoresis experiment and the role that the gel plays in that experiment. The question states that the proteins being analyzed are denatured, which means they have lost any tertiary or quaternary structure the protein once had. This eliminates choices A and B. You need to also recall that during electrophoresis, all of the denatured proteins are coated by this SDS molecule, meaning they are all relatively equal in their solubility in water. Thus, you can determine that in SDS-gel electrophoresis, the proteins will be separated only by molecular weight. As a result of this work, choice D is correct.

Task 4 Data-Based and Statistical Reasoning

The last task for the new MCAT is really not that new. Interpreting figures, tables, graphs and equations has been a necessary skill in reading passages efficiently as you read about in earlier in this book. With these six questions (on average), the test will make this task more formal. To succeed you must train yourself to be able to deduce patterns in data presented in graphs tables and figures. It will also ask you to draw conclusions based on the scientific data given in a passage or question.

Task 4 Example Question

10. Nitric oxide has been shown to be an important molecule that can affect blood pressure by initiating vasodilation. Nitric oxide can also react with elemental oxygen in the gas phase to form nitrogen dioxide, which has a toxic effect on the body. The following data was collected concerning three blood tests run on a patient in the ER.

Test	[NO] (mol/L)	[O_2] (mol/L)	[NO_2] (mol/L)
1	5.3×10^{-6}	1.1×10^{-2}	8.2×10^{-3}
2	4.7×10^{-3}	1.1×10^{-2}	1.5×10^{-4}
3	2.6×10^{-2}	1.1×10^{-2}	1.1×10^{-5}

During which test is arterial radius expected to be the largest?

A) Test 1

B) Test 2

C) Test 3

D) All tests would give the same measurement result

This is a task 4 question because to answer it, you must consult the table of experimental data as well as understand the role of NO in the circulatory system. In humans, NO is a signaling molecule involved that is a powerful vasodilator with a short half-life of a few seconds in the blood. Thus, the greatest concentration of NO would cause the largest increase in blood vessel dilation, which is the expansion or widening of blood vessels. Examining the data you can see that test 3 showed the highest levels of NO in the blood. Thus, choice C is correct.

Use the four passages on the following pages as a way to practice your highlighting technique and your problem solving ability. You want to get comfortable with the different question types on the exam. For now, don't worry about time. Speed will come with practice.

Passage 1 (Questions 11-15)

A DNA polymerase is an enzyme that catalyzes the formation of a strand of nucleotides based on a DNA template. During the S phase of the cell cycle, two copies of DNA polymerase act on the existing genetic material to create two new copies. The process of DNA replication however, requires much more than the presence of DNA polymerase. The many enzymes involved and their function are outlined in figure 1.

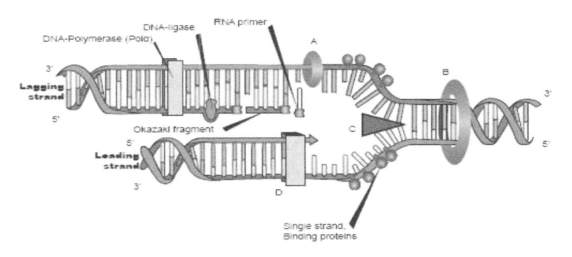

Figure-1: *A schematic of DNA replication with all of the enzymes involved*

The function of DNA polymerase is simply to read a single strand of DNA and add the correct nucleotide to complement the template. DNA polymerase can only add new nucleotides to the 3' end of the strand being synthesized. DNA polymerases make about one mistake per billion nucleotides added. Most DNA polymerases have the built-in ability to recognize and correct these mistakes when they occur. When mistakes occur, the offending base is cleaved out of the strand by enzymes and DNA polymerase will add the correct base. After this, DNA ligase connects the loose ends.

DNA ligase catalyzes the joining together of two DNA strands by forming a phosphodiester bond between the two strands. DNA ligase first binds an AMP molecule to a lysine residue in its structure. This AMP is attacked by the 5' phosphate group between the nucleotides, transferring the AMP to the phosphate group. The addition of the AMP to the 5' phosphate makes the phosphorous atom more susceptible to attack by the 3' OH group of the next nucleotide. The attack results in the release of AMP and H_2O and the formation of a phosphodiester bond.

Figure-2: *AMP*

11. If there are 6 billion base pairs in a diploid cell, how many errors will occur on average during DNA replication in that cell?

A) 3

B) 6

C) 9

D) 12

12. If the following DNA strand is being opened and replicated from right to left, which strand will be the lagging strand?

5' AGTCTCCGGATTAACGATGC 3'
| | | | | | | | | | | | | | | | | | | |
3' TCAGAGGCCTAATTGCTACG 5'

A) The top strand will be the lagging strand because DNA polymerase will be adding nucleotides in the 3' direction from left to right on the top strand.

B) The top strand will be the lagging strand because DNA polymerase will be adding nucleotides in the 3' direction from right to left on the top strand.

C) The bottom strand will be the lagging strand because DNA polymerase will be adding nucleotides in the 3' direction from left to right on the bottom strand.

D) The bottom strand will be the lagging strand because DNA polymerase will be adding nucleotides in the 3' direction from right to left on the bottom strand.

13. Which of the following represents the bond formation between adjacent nucleotides being joined by DNA ligase?

14. Which of the following labeled enzymes on figure 1 is primase?

A) A   B) B
C) C   D) D

15. Which of the following best describes the effect of addition of AMP to a phosphate group?
   A) AMP is electron donating and contributes to the phosphate's nucleophilic affinity.
   B) AMP is electron donating and contributes to the phosphorus atom's electrophilic nature.
   C) AMP is electron withdrawing.
   D) AMP is electron donating and contributes to the phosphorus atom's electronegativity.

Passage 1 Explanation

A **DNA polymerase** is an enzyme that catalyzes the formation of a strand of nucleotides based on a DNA **template**. During the **S phase** of the cell cycle, two copies of DNA polymerase act on the existing genetic material to create two new copies. The process of **DNA replication** however, requires much more than the presence of DNA polymerase. The many enzymes involved and their function are outlined in figure 1.

Key Terms: DNA polymerase, template, S phase, DNA replication.

Cause and effect: This first paragraph tells us that DNA polymerase is the enzyme that creates new DNA from an existing template. We are told a little about how this process occurs.

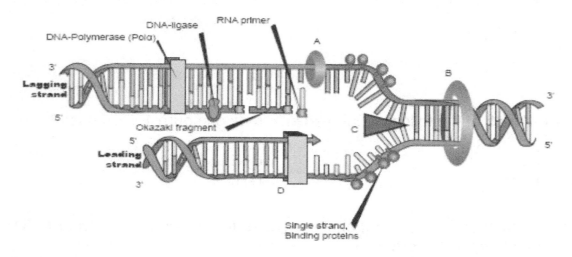

Figure-1: *A schematic of DNA replication with all of the enzymes involved*

Figure-1: Shows the enzymes involved in DNA replication and where their action takes place.

The function of DNA polymerase is simply to read a single strand of DNA and add the correct nucleotide to complement the template. DNA polymerase can only add new nucleotides to the **3' end** of the strand being synthesized. DNA polymerases make about **one mistake per billion** nucleotides added. Most DNA polymerases have the built in ability to recognize and correct these mistakes when they occur. When mistakes occur, the offending base is cleaved out of the strand by enzymes and DNA polymerase will add the correct base. After this, **DNA ligase** connects the loose ends.

Key Terms: 3' end, one mistake per billion nucleotides, DNA ligase.

Cause and effect: We are told a little more about the function of DNA polymerase and how nucleotides are added. We are told that mistakes do occur and that DNA ligase is involved in connecting a break in a strand of DNA that might occur during nucleotide repair.

DNA ligase catalyzes the joining together of two DNA strands by forming a **phosphodiester bond** between the two strands. DNA ligase first binds an **AMP molecule** to a **lysine** residue in its structure. This AMP is attacked by the **5' phosphate group** between the nucleotides, transferring the AMP to the phosphate group. The addition of the AMP to the 5' phosphate makes the phosphorous atom more **susceptible to attack** by the *3' OH* group of the next nucleotide. The attack results in the release of AMP and H_2O and the formation of a phosphodiester bond.

Key Terms: phosphodiester bond, AMP molecule, lysine, 5' phosphate group, 3' OH.

Cause and effect: We are told about the function of DNA ligase and how it brings about the ligation of two adjacent nucleotides. It uses an AMP intermediate to catalyze the 3' OH attack of the adjacent 5' phosphate group.

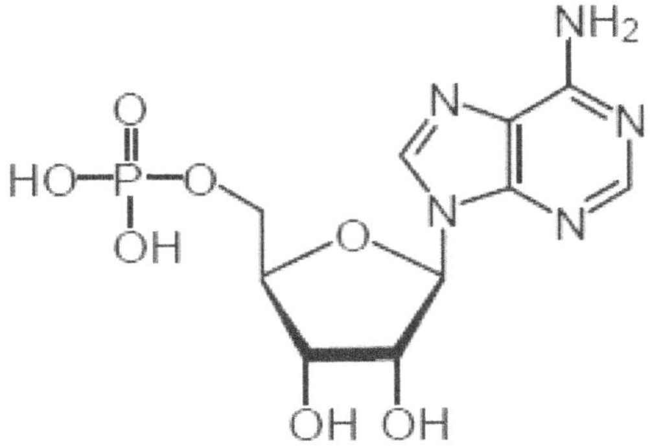

Figure-2: *AMP*

Figure-2: Shows the structure of AMP, which is used in the mechanism of DNA ligase.

11. If there are 6 billion base pairs in a diploid cell, how many errors will occur on average during DNA replication in that cell?

A) 3

B) 6

C) 9

D) 12

Answer: D. The passage states that 1 mistake will occur per billion nucleotides added on average. If the genome has 6 billion base pairs and we are making a copy of it, then we will need to add 12 billion bases. Thus choice D is correct.

12. If the following DNA strand is being opened and replicated from right to left, which strand will be the lagging strand?

5' AGTCTCCGGATTAACGATGC 3'
| | | | | | | | | | | | | | | | | | | |
3' TCAGAGGCCTAATTGCTACG 5'

A) The top strand will be the lagging strand because DNA polymerase will be adding nucleotides in the 3' direction from left to right on the top strand.

B) The top strand will be the lagging strand because DNA polymerase will be adding nucleotides in the 3' direction from right to left on the top strand.

C) The bottom strand will be the lagging strand because DNA polymerase will be adding nucleotides in the 3' direction from left to right on the bottom strand.

D) The bottom strand will be the lagging strand because DNA polymerase will be adding nucleotides in the 3' direction from right to left on the bottom strand.

Answer: C. This question asks us to consider the fact that DNA polymerase must add nucleotides on the 3' side of the strand being synthesized. This means that it will synthesize in the direction of the 5' end of the template strand. Thus, if the DNA is opening at the right, the bottom strand will be the lagging strand where Okazaki fragments are formed. Thus choice C is correct.

13. Which of the following represents the bond formation between adjacent nucleotides being joined by DNA ligase?

Answer: C. This question asks us to interpret what is stated in the last paragraph. The paragraph states that the 3' OH group of one nucleotide attacks the 5' phosphorus of the next. Since we are dealing with DNA, the 2 carbon should not have a OH group attached. Thus choice D is correct.

A, C: The phosphate does not attack a carbon.

B: This is an RNA molecule attacking the phosphate.

14. Which of the following labeled enzymes on figure 1 is primase?

A) A   B) B
C) C   D) D

Answer: A. This question requires outside knowledge. DNA primase adds an RNA primer to which DNA polymerase can begin working. Thus choice A is correct.

B: This is topoisomerase.

C: This is helicase.

D: This is DNA polymerase.

15. Which of the following best describes the effect of addition of AMP to a phosphate group?

A) AMP is electron donating and contributes to the phosphate's nucleophilic affinity.

B) AMP is electron donating and contributes to the phosphorus atom's electrophilic nature.

C) AMP is electron withdrawing.

D) AMP is electron donating and contributes to the phosphorus atom's electronegativity.

Answer: C. This question asks us to interpret what is stated in the last paragraph. The paragraph states that the addition of AMP to the 5' phosphate group makes it susceptible to attack by OH which is a nucleophile. This means that the phosphate group becomes less electron rich. This can only occur if AMP is withdrawing electron density from the 5' phosphate group. Thus choice C is the correct answer.

A, B, and D: AMP cannot be adding electron density to the phosphate group because it is being attacked by a nucleophile.

Passage 2 (Questions 16-20)

Secretin is secreted by the small intestine in response to lowered pH. Secretin is a linear peptide hormone.

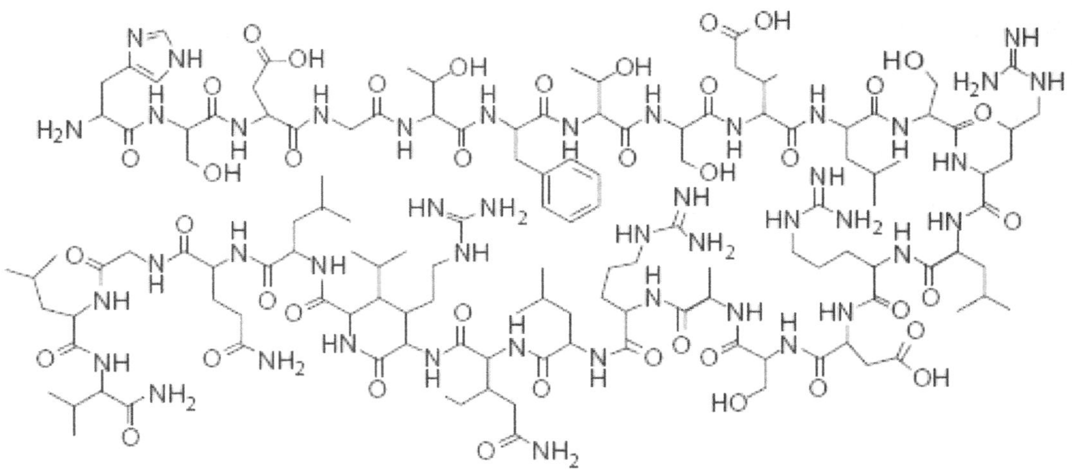

Figure-1: *The structure of secretin*

Cholecystokinin is anenzyme whose action is enhanced by the presence of secretin. Cholecystokinin is secreted from the duodenum when fat reaches the small intestine. Cholecystokinin stimulates contraction of the gallbladder and stimulates the pancreas to secrete enzymes to aid in digestion. The following enzymes are released by the pancreas:

Table 1 Some enzymes in pancreatic juice and their function	
Enzyme	Function
Lipase	Break down fats
Nuclease	Break phosphodiester bonds
Trypsinogen ➔ trypsin	Break down proteins
Chymotrypsinogen ➔ chymotrypsin	Break down proteins
Amylase	Break down starches
Procarboxypeptidase ➔ carboxypeptidase	Break down peptides

Trypsinogen, chymotrypsinogen and procarboxypeptidase are zymogens, inactive forms of enzymes. They are activated by trypsin, which is itself the active form of the zymogen trypsinogen. Trypsinogen can be formed into trypsin by the enzyme enterokinase, which is released from the cells of the duodenum.

Amylase, nuclease, and lipase are able to directly catalyze the metabolism of certain molecules. Amylase functions to break down starch, a polymer of glucose molecules.

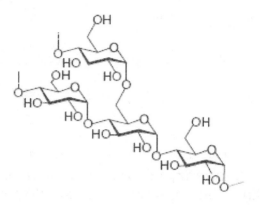

Figure-2: *A starch molecule*

Amylase breaks down starches into maltose subunits. Maltose is a disaccharide composed of two glucose units joined in an α(1-4) glycosidic linkage.

16. How does the small intestine know to release secretin only after a meal?

   A) The increase in hydrogen ions from the breakdown of peptides and carbohydrates lowers the pH in the small intestine.

   B) The release of hydrochloric acid in the stomach lowers the pH in the small intestine.

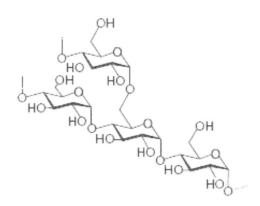

C) Acetic acid, a byproduct of carbohydrate digestion, lowers the pH in the small intestine.

D) The release of bile acids lowers the pH in the small intestine.

17. Which of the following, if absent, would lead to the biggest decrease in our ability to digest proteins?

A) Chymotrypsinogen   B) Chymotrypsin
C) Carboxypeptidase   D) Enterokinase

18. Which of the following enzymes catalyzes the reaction below?

A) Sucrase
B) Lactase
C) Maltase
D) Lipase

19. Which of the following is the structure of maltose?

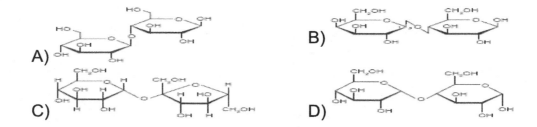

20. Which of the following is true concerning secretin?

A) Secretin is unique because the carboxyl-terminal amino acid is an amide.

B) Secretin is unique because it contains equal amounts of basic and acidic side groups.

C) Secretin is unique because the amine-terminal residue contains a basic side group.

D) Secretin is unique because the carboxyl-terminal residue is hydrophobic.

Passage 2 Explanation

Secretin is secreted by the small intestine in response to lowered pH. Secretin is a linear **peptide hormone**.

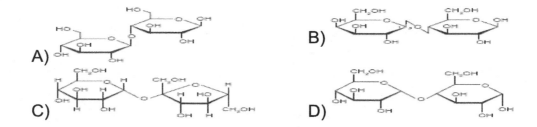

Figure-1: *The structure of secretin*

104

Figure-1: Shows the amino acid sequence of secretin

Cholecystokinin is an enzyme whose action is enhanced by the presence of secretin. Cholecystokinin is secreted from the **duodenum** when fat reaches the small intestine. Cholecystokinin stimulates contraction of the **gallbladder** and stimulates the **pancreas** to secrete enzymes to aid in digestion. The following enzymes are released by the pancreas:

Key Terms: secretin, peptide hormone, cholecystokinin, duodenum, gallbladder, pancreas. This first section of the passage tells us about secretin and its action to promote cholecystokinin.

Cause and Effect: secretin enhances the action of cholecystokinin. Cholecystokinin causes contraction of the gallbladder. Cholecystokinin causes secretion of pancreatic enzymes.

Table 1 Some enzymes in pancreatic juice and their function	
Enzyme	Function
Lipase	Break down fats
Nuclease	Break phosphodiester bonds
Trypsinogen → trypsin	Break down proteins
Chymotrypsinogen → chymotrypsin	Break down proteins
Amylase	Break down starches
Procarboxypeptidase → carboxypeptidase	Break down peptides

Trypsinogen, chymotrypsinogen and procarboxypeptidase are **zymogens**, inactive forms of enzymes. They are activated by **trypsin**, which is itself the active form of the zymogen trypsinogen. Trypsinogen can be formed into trypsin by the enzyme **enterokinase**, which is released from the cells of the duodenum.

Key Terms: trypsinogen, chymotrypsinogen, procarboxypeptidase, zymogens, trypsin, enterokinase. We are told in this paragraph about zymogens and how they are activated to begin digestion of food.

Cause and Effect: enterokinase catalyzes the formation of trypsin from trypsinogen. Trypsin catalyzes the activation of all other zymogens in pancreatic juice.

Amylase, nuclease, and lipase are able to directly catalyze the metabolism of certain molecules. Amylase function to break down **starch**, a polymer of glucose molecules.

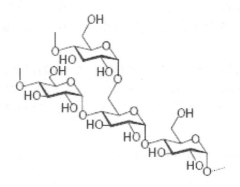

Figure-2: *a starch molecule*

Amylase breaks down starches into **maltose** subunits. Maltose is a disaccharide composed of two glucose units joined in an **α(1-4) glycosidic linkage**.

Key Terms: amylase, nuclease, lipase, starch, maltose, α(1-4) glycosidic linkage.

Cause and effect: The last section tells us about amylase and its function. We learn what a maltose disaccharide looks like.

16. How does the small intestine know to release secretin only after a meal?

A) The increase in hydrogen ions from the breakdown of peptides and carbohydrates lowers the pH in the small intestine.

B) **The release of hydrochloric acid in the stomach lowers the pH in the small intestine.**

106

C) Acetic acid, a byproduct of carbohydrate digestion, lowers the pH in the small intestine.

D) The release of bile acids lowers the pH in the small intestine.

Answer: B. This question asks us to consider why the pH of the small intestine will decrease after a meal. The reason is that the stomach releases hydrochloric acid so that the chyme entering the small intestine is acidic. Thus choice B is correct.

A: The breakdown of macronutrients doesn't lower the pH.

C: Acetic acid is not a byproduct of carbohydrate digestion.

D: The release of bile acids would lower the pH but secretin is one of the first things secreted and promotes the secretion of bile acids.

17. Which of the following, if absent, would lead to the biggest decrease in our ability to digest proteins?

A) Chymotrypsinogen   B) Chymotrypsin
C) Carboxypeptidase   **D) Enterokinase**

Answer: D. Remember that enterokinase activates trypsin which activates all the other zymogens that break down proteins. Thus choice D is correct.

18. Which of the following enzymes catalyzes the reaction below?

A) **Sucrase**   B) Lactase
C) Maltase   D) Lipase

Answer: A. Remember that a glucose linked to a fructose is a sucrose molecule. It makes sense that sucrase is the enzyme that catalyzes this reaction. Thus choice A is correct.

B: Lactase catalyzes the breakdown of lactose into glucose and galactose.

C: Maltase catalyzes the breakdown of maltose into two glucose molecules.

D: Lipase catalyzes the breakdown of fats.

19. Which of the following is the structure of maltose?

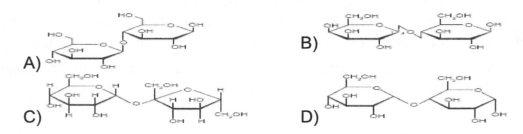

A)

B)

C)

D)

Answer: D. The passage states that maltose consists of two glucose molecules with an α(1-4) glycosidic linkage. Thus choice D is correct.

A: This is a beta linkage.

B: This is a beta linkage between galactose and glucose

C: This contains a fructose

20. Which of the following is true concerning secretin?

A)
Secretin is unique because the carboxyl-terminal amino acid is an amide.

B)
Secretin is unique because it contains equal amounts of basic and acidic side groups

C)
Secretin is unique because the amine-terminal residue contains a basic side group

D)
Secretin is unique because the carboxyl-terminal residue is hydrophobic

Answer: A. This question requires us to consider figure 1. Normally, the carboxyl terminal amino acid ends in a carboxylic acid. Secretin ends in an amide (which is a carbonyl group attached to a nitrogen group). Thus choice A is correct.

B: This is not true of secretin.

C, D: This is not unique to secretin.

Passage 3 (Questions 21-25)

Muscle contraction is a complicated process with many steps. It all begins with an action potential that is transmitted along a motor neuron towards muscle tissue. Efferent somatic neurons use the neurotransmitter acetylcholine.

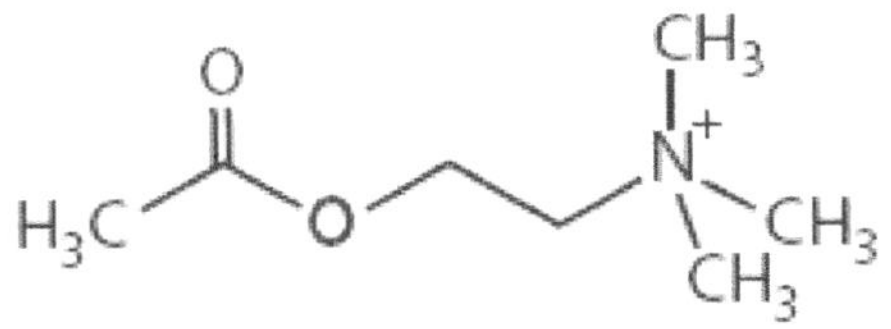

A 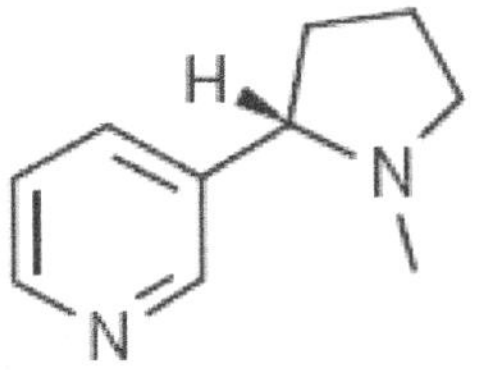   B

Figure-1: *Acetylcholine (A) and nicotine (B)*

When the action potential reaches a muscle cell, known as a sarcomere, acetylcholine is released and binds a nicotinic acetylcholine receptor on the neuromuscular junction. Nicotinic receptors are so named because they also bind nicotine. When this receptor is activated, it causes depolarization of the sarcomere and an electrochemical signal is transduced along the muscle fiber, depolarizing all the sarcomeres in the fiber. When a sarcomere is depolarized, calcium channels in the cell's membrane open, which in turn opens the calcium channels of the sarcoplasmic reticulum and calcium rushes into the cytoplasm of the muscle cells.

The actual contraction of muscle occurs as a result of calcium binding troponin C, a compound found on thin actin filaments. The binding of calcium to troponin C causes tropomyosin, which normally blocks binding sites on the thin filaments, to move. The binding sites are exposed and thick filament myosin heads can interact with thin filaments, pulling them toward the M line.

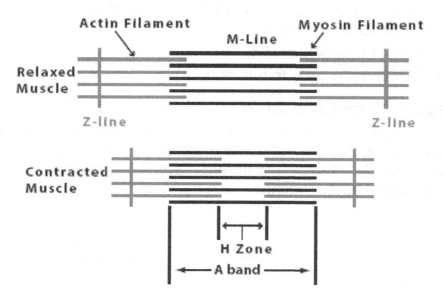

Figure-2: *The filaments in a sarcomere and how they move when the sarcomere contracts*

Myosin can freely bind the thin filaments. Myosin at this stage is also bound to an ADP and inorganic phosphate group, which when released, cause the stroke and pulling inward toward the M line. When ATP binds myosin, myosin releases the thin filaments and the ATP is hydrolyzed, allowing the myosin to revert to its original state, ready to bind another binding site on the actin fibers. Each stroke moves the thin filaments about 10 nm closer to the M-line.

21. Which of the following shortens during the contraction of two adjacent sarcomeres?

I. Length of H zone

II. Distance between Z lines

III. Distance between M lines

A) I only

B) I and II only

C) II and III only

D) I, II, and III

22. Which of the following would result in paralysis of skeletal muscle?
   A) A peptide hormone that agonistically binds nicotinic acetylcholine receptors
   B) A peptide hormone that antagonistically binds muscarinic receptors
   C) A peptide hormone that antagonistically binds nicotinic acetylcholine receptors
   D) A peptide hormone that agonistically binds muscarinic receptors

23. How many sets of power strokes in myosin filaments are required to shorten a sarcomere by 80 nm?

   A) 4
   C) 16

   B) 8
   D) it depends on the length of the sarcomere

24. Which of the following is LEAST likely to be able to bind a nicotinic receptor?

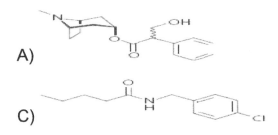

25. Which of the following must be present in abundance for skeletal muscle contraction to begin?

   I. Calcium
   III. ATP
   A) III only
   C) I and III only

   II. ADP

   B) I and II only
   D) II and III only

Passage 3 Explanation

Muscle contraction is a complicated process with many steps. It all begins with an action potential that is transmitted along a motor neuron towards muscle tissue. **Efferent somatic neurons** use the neurotransmitter **acetylcholine**.

Key Terms: muscle contraction, efferent somatic neurons, acetylcholine. This paragraph tells us that acetylcholine is used as the neurotransmitter to skeletal muscle.

Figure-1: *Acetylcholine (left) and nicotine (right)*

Figure-1: Acetylcholine (left) and nicotine (right) shows the structures of acetylcholine and nicotine, which bind nicotinic acetylcholine receptors

When the action potential reaches a muscle cell, known as a **sarcomere**, acetylcholine is released and binds a **nicotinic acetylcholine receptor** on the neuromuscular junction. Nicotinic receptors are so named because they also bind **nicotine**. When this receptor is activated, it causes depolarization of the sarcomere and an electrochemical signal is transduced along the muscle fiber, depolarizing all the sarcomeres in the fiber. When a sarcomere is depolarized, **calcium channels** in the cell's membrane open, which in turn opens the calcium channels of the **sarcoplasmic reticulum** and calcium rushes into the cytoplasm of the muscle cells.

Key Terms: sarcomere, nicotinic acetylcholine receptor, nicotine, calcium channels, sarcoplasmic reticulum. This paragraph tells us how the process of contraction begins.

Cause and Effect: the binding of acetylcholine opens voltage gated channels. This opens calcium voltage gated channels. This opens calcium voltage gated channels in the sarcoplasmic reticulum. This increases the calcium ion concentration of the cell dramatically.

The actual contraction of muscle occurs as a result of calcium binding **troponin C**, a compound found on **thin actin filaments**. The binding of calcium to troponin C causes **tropomyosin**, which normally blocks binding sites on the thin filaments, to move. The binding sites are exposed and thick filament **myosin** heads can interact with thin filaments, pulling them toward the **M line**.

Key Terms: troponin C, thin actin filaments, tropomyosin, myosin, M-line. This paragraph is a continuation of the last, explaining the process of muscle contraction.

Cause and Effect: calcium binding troponin C causes tropomyosin to move, which allows for myosin head to bind actin filaments.

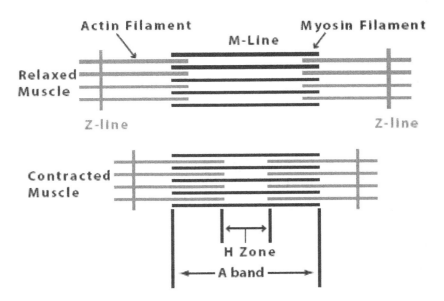

Figure-2: *A diagram of the filaments in a sarcomere and how they move when the sarcomere contracts. Shows how a sarcomere changes after contraction.*

Figure-2: Shows how a sarcomere changes after contraction.

Myosin can freely bind the thin filaments. Myosin at this stage is also bound to an **ADP and inorganic phosphate** group, which when released, cause the stroke and pulling inward toward the M line. When ATP binds myosin, myosin releases the thin filaments and the **ATP** is hydrolyzed, allowing the myosin to revert to its original state, ready to bind another binding site on the actin fibers. Each stroke moves the thin filaments about *10 nm* closer to the M-line.

Key Terms: ADP, inorganic phosphate, ATP, 10 nm. This last paragraph finishes the explanation of muscle contraction.

Cause and Effect: When ADP and P$_i$ are removed from myosin, the power stroke occurs. When ATP binds myosin, it release the thin filaments.

21. Which of the following shortens during the contraction of two adjacent sarcomeres?
I. Length of H zone
II. Distance between Z lines
III. Distance between M lines

A) I only   B) I and II only
II and III only   D) I, II, and III

Answer: D. Remember that the Z-lines are being brought closer together and that the actin filaments are being brought closer together. M lines are brought closer together because each sarcomere is shortened. This means that choice D is correct.

22. Which of the following would result in paralysis of skeletal muscle?
A) a peptide hormone that agonistically binds nicotinic acetylcholine receptors
B) a peptide hormone that antagonistically binds muscarinic receptors
C) a peptide hormone that antagonistically binds nicotinic acetylcholine receptors
D) a peptide hormone that agonistically binds muscarinic receptors

114

Answer: C. Paralysis of skeletal muscle will occur if the function of nicotinic acetylcholine receptors is interrupted. An antagonist is a molecule that interrupts the normal function of another enzyme or receptor. Thus choice C is correct.

23. How many sets of power strokes in myosin filaments are required to shorten a sarcomere by 80 nm?

A) 4
B) 8
C) 16
D) it depends on the length of the sarcomere

Answer: A. The passage states that each actin filament is moved 10 nm per power stroke. Since there are actin filaments on both sides of the Z line in figure 2, we require only a 40 nm movement on either side. Thus choice A is correct.

24. Which of the following is LEAST likely to be able to bind a nicotinic receptor?

Answer: C. We are given two examples of molecules that bind nicotinic receptors in figure 1. Choice C is unlike either example and does not have a tertiary amine. Thus choice C is the best answer.

A: This molecule has a tertiary amine group just like nicotine

B: This molecule has a quaternary ammonium ion just like acetylcholine.

D: This molecule has a tertiary amine group just like nicotine

25. Which of the following must be present in abundance for skeletal muscle contraction to begin?

I. Calcium II. ADP
III. ATP
A) III only B) I and II only
C) I and III D) II, and III

Answer: C. The passage states (and you should know from outside knowledge) that muscles need Ca^{2+} ions to contract. Once calcium binds to troponin, it causes a conformational shift in the tropomyosin protein. This shift exposes myosin binding sites on actin, which allows the actin-myosin cross links to form, which causes the filaments to slide over each other, causing contraction. Additionally, we need ATP to remove myosin from actin filaments. Thus choice C is correct.

A, B, D: ADP, is the product of ATP hydrolysis and is not the energy source required for the muscle power stroke. We do not need ADP because ATP is hydrolyzed to ADP and P_i after binding myosin.

Passage 4 (Questions 26-30)

Erythropoiesis is the process by which new red blood cells are created in the body. The average red blood cell will circulate for about 120 days, after which time they undergo apoptosis.

The process begins with the secretion of the hormone erythropoietin from the kidney. The kidney contains chemoreceptors that react to a drop in O_2 partial pressure in circulating blood. In response to a hypoxic environment, kidney cells produce erythropoietin.

Once erythropoietin is produced and secreted it targets cells in bone marrow to direct the formation of erythrocyte precursors from hematopoietic stem cells. A hematopoietic stem cell is a cell isolated from the blood or bone marrow that can renew itself, can differentiate to a variety of specialized cells, can mobilize out of the bone marrow into circulating blood, and can undergo programmed cell death. Once the cell reaches the stage of reticulocyte, it has only to increase production of hemoglobin to become an erythrocyte. The percent of reticulocytes in circulation is a good indicator of the level of new erythrocytes creation. Normally reticulocytes form around 1% of all red blood cells.

Red blood cell count needs to be carefully regulated so that complications do not arise from having too few or too many red blood cells in circulation at a given time. The fact that erythropoietin binds red blood cells while in circulation means that even in large amounts, erythropoietin will not act unless there is a significant reduction of erythrocyte count. Hepcidin is a peptide hormone that inhibits iron release from macrophages in bone marrow, making it impossible to form the heme group necessary for erythrocyte function. Increased levels of hepcidin therefore coincide with decreased hematocrit. Hepcidin also acts as an inhibitor of ferroportin, which transports iron from the gut into the body.

26. If a person donates blood on January 1, on which day are they most likely to have elevated amounts of erythropoietin in circulation?

A) February 6   B) March 4
C) May 2   D) July 1

27. Under which of the following categories does blood fall?

A) Heart tissue   B) Lymph tissue
C) Kidney tissue   D) Connective tissue

28. Which of the following might result from living at high elevation?
A) Clogged arteries
B) Greater plasma volume
C) Reduced hematocrit
D) Decreased hepcidin production

29. Which of the following would lead to reticulocyte count of 0.4%?
A) Increased ferroportin activity
B) Decreased hepcidin activity
C) An increase in blood temperature

D) An increase in blood pH

30. If each erythrocyte contains 2.8×10^8 hemoglobin molecules and there are 2.5×10^{13} erythrocytes in circulation, how many grams of iron are in circulation?

A) 0.7 grams   B) 2.6 grams
C) 7 grams   D) 10.4 grams

Passage 4 Explanation

Erythropoiesis is the process by which new **red blood cells** are created in the body. The average red blood cell will circulate for about **120 days**, after which time they undergo **apoptosis**.

Key Terms: Erythropoiesis, red blood cells, 120 days, apoptosis.

Cause & effect: We are told what erythropoiesis is and how long erythrocytes live in circulation.

The process begins with the secretion of the hormone **erythropoietin** from the **kidney**. The kidney contains **chemoreceptors** that react to a drop in **O_2 partial pressure** in circulating blood. In response to a *hypoxic* environment, kidney cells produce erythropoietin.

Key Terms: erythropoietin, kidney, chemoreceptors, O_2 partial pressure, hypoxic. This paragraph tells us that the kidney plays a key role in erythropoiesis by releasing erythropoietin.

Cause and Effect: decreased O_2 partial pressure leads to erythropoietin secretion.

Once erythropoietin is produced and secreted it targets cells in **bone marrow** to direct the formation of **erythrocyte** precursors from hematopoietic stem cells. A **hematopoietic stem cell** is a cell isolated from the blood or bone marrow that can renew itself, can differentiate to a variety of specialized cells, can mobilize out of the bone marrow into circulating blood, and can undergo programmed cell death. Once the cell reaches the stage of **reticulocyte**, it has only to increase production of hemoglobin to become an erythrocyte. The percent of reticulocytes in circulation is a good indicator of the level of new erythrocyte creation. Normally reticulocytes form around **1%** of all red blood cells.

Key Terms: bone marrow, erythrocyte precursors, hematopoietic stem cells, reticulocyte, 1%.

Cause & effect: We are told in this paragraph that erythropoietin targets stem cells in bone marrow to direct the formation of erythrocytes. Reticulocytes are precursors of erythrocytes and are about 1% of all red blood cells in circulation.

Cause and Effect: the number of reticulocytes in circulation indicates the level at which erythropoiesis has been taking place.

Red blood cell count needs to be carefully regulated so that complications do not arise from having too few or too many red blood cells in circulation at a given time. The fact that erythropoietin binds red blood cells while in circulation means that even in large amounts, erythropoietin will not act unless there is a significant reduction of erythrocyte count. **Hepcidin** is a peptide hormone that inhibits iron release from **macrophages** in bone marrow, making it impossible to form the **heme** group necessary for erythrocyte function. Increased levels of hepcidin therefore coincide with decreased hematocrit. Hepcidin also acts as an inhibitor of **ferroportin**, which transports iron from the gut into the body.

Key Terms: hepcidin, macrophages, heme, ferroportin. We are told in this paragraph about some of the control mechanisms the body has to regulate hematocrit.

Cause and Effect: hepcidin inhibits erythropoiesis, ferroportin allows it to take place.

26. If a person donates blood on January 1, on which day are they most likely to have elevated amounts of erythropoietin in circulation?

A) February 6   March 4

C) May 2   D) July 1

Answer: C. The passages states that erythrocytes live for about 4 months. If you donated blood on January 1, you would have an immediate increase in erythropoietin to create red blood cells and make up for your loss. However, the influx of red blood cells will all die at about the same time, 4 months from January 1. If this is true, those cells would die around May 2 and we would need an influx of erythropoietin. Choice C is the best answer.

27. Under which of the following categories does blood fall?

   A) Heart tissue   B) Lymph tissue
   C) Kidney tissue   D) Connective tissue

Answer: D. Blood is connective tissue. Thus choice D is correct.

28. Which of the following might result from living at high elevation?
   A) Clogged arteries
   B) Greater plasma volume
   C) Reduced hematocrit
   D) Decreased hepcidin production

Answer: A. At a high elevation, oxygen is less abundant. This means that the kidney will be signaled to release more erythropoietin, resulting in more red blood cells. Red blood cells are the heaviest and thickest part of blood. An increased hematocrit can lead to more viscous blood and arteries that are more easily clogged. Thus choice A is correct.

   B: There is no reason to think that plasma volume will increase if red blood cell count increases.
   C: There will be an increased hematocrit
   D: Hepcidin is an antagonist of erythropoiesis, thus we can expect higher levels of hepcidin if red blood cell count becomes abnormally high.

29. Which of the following would lead to reticulocyte count of 0.4%?

A) Increased ferroportin activity

B) Decreased hepcidin activity

C) An increase in blood temperature

D) An increase in blood pH

Answer: D. Remember that an increase in blood pH results in a greater binding affinity of hemoglobin for oxygen. This means that the kidney will read higher levels of oxygen in the blood and release less erythropoietin, resulting in a lower reticulocyte count. Thus choice D is correct.

A: Increased ferroportin activity will lend itself to the creation of more reticulocytes

B: Decreased hepcidin activity will allow for increased creation of reticulocytes

C: An increase in blood temperature shifts the hemoglobin binding curve to the right, meaning that there will be less oxygen in the blood at the kidneys and they will release erythropoietin, resulting in a higher reticulocyte count.

30. If each erythrocyte contains 2.8×10^8 hemoglobin molecules and there are 2.5×10^{13} erythrocytes in circulation, how many grams of iron are in circulation?

A) 0.7 grams

B) 2.6 grams

C) 7 grams

D) 10.4 grams

Answer: B. First we multiply 2.8×10^8 by 2.5×10^{13} to get 7×10^{21} hemoglobin molecules in circulation, each one contains four heme groups with one iron ion per heme. This means we have $7.4 \times 10^{21} = 2.8 \times 10^{22}$ Fe atoms. Divide by Avogadro's number. We can approximate $2.8/6.022 = .5$ so we get 0.5×10^{-1} mol Fe. Multiply this by 56 grams/mole to get 2.8 grams of Fe. This is closest to choice B, which is the correct answer.

CHAPTER 13
CARS SECTION PASSAGE STRATEGIES

Some people will try to tell you that there's a single "best" way to do the CARS section of the MCAT. Needless to say, that's wrong. There are as many different right approaches as there are test-takers. After all, everyone's brain works a little differently. So the first thing you want to do is to find an approach that makes the most sense *for you*.

To that end, we're going to discuss three different approaches to the passages. You should start by practicing these approaches to find one that suits you best. Then, start to make adjustments as needed as you practice more.

To begin with, let's discuss two major factors: the tools at your disposal and how to allocate time.

First, on test day you have two simple tools to deal with the CARS passages: **your marker** and booklet, and the **highlighting function** on the screen. You're going to need to decide how to use these tools to best effect. Some people like stopping while reading and jotting some notes down. Others like to highlight while they read, but not take any notes. Finally, some people like to just whiz through the passage as quickly as possible without using either the marker or the highlighter.

How should you use these tools?

Marker and booklet: only stop to jot down important ideas. Avoid an overly mechanical approach. Instead, jot down the connections between important ideas as they come up. For some paragraphs, you may write nothing, since there's no important notes. By contrast, other paragraphs may require a bunch of notes.

Highlighter: use this sparingly. If you highlight everything, then you end up highlighting nothing. Don't highlight big chunks of text just "because it looks important". Instead, pick out individual words that capture the author's most important ideas. Highlight key terms, contrasts, opinions, cause-and-effect relationships.

Key terms:	Any proper nouns that look important. Names, dates, other technical terms that you want to be able to find again quickly. For example, Isaac Newton, post-1989, categorical imperative, CDC.
Opinions:	Most importantly, the author's opinion. This can mean the opinion of a person, or of an entire school of thought. For example, "Postmodernism fundamentally rejects a static, universal view of science" is just as much an opinion as, "Picasso found his early work to be too constrained and 'adult-looking'."
Contrast:	Any contrasts that show up between people, ideas, cultures, etc. For example: old vs. new, author vs. art critic, French vs. Vietnamese, radical vs. conservative.
Cause and effect:	For the purposes of this book, we are using the term "cause and effect" in a very loose, rhetorical sense. We're referring to any connections between ideas that have a because-therefore relationship. For example, "The existence of a successful democracy

depends upon high-quality free public education," "The initial step in the formation of a dental cavity is adherence of the lactic acid secreting bacteria to the enamel of the tooth, following by plaque deposition," and "Rising income levels have a direct correlation with civic engagement as measured by voting behavior."

How should you allocate your time?

You will have approximately 10 minutes to read a passage, analyze its content, and answer all of the questions that go with it. Broadly speaking, you can spend that time in three ways: mainly on the questions, mainly on the passage, or split evenly between them.

The most common approach, and the one that is most successful for more students, is an even-split approach. Spend about 4 to 4.5 minutes reading the passage, and then 5.5 to 6 minutes answering the questions. This way you have enough time to carefully consider the ideas presented in the text, while still having enough time to occasionally go back and look up materials to help you answer the questions.

However, some students find that they're not ever comfortable answering a question unless they go back and look something up in the passage. For those students, they should move quickly through the passage (only 1.5 minutes) and then spend the bulk of their time very carefully analyzing each question and looking for support in the passage.

Finally, a student with an exceptional short-term memory may find it better to slow down on the passage, read each sentence and paragraph two (or even three) times in order to really "master" the passage over the course of six or seven minutes. That only leaves 2 – 3 minutes to move very quickly through the questions.

Now that we've looked at the different tools you have available and seen three possible ways to spend your time on the test, let's discuss the three possible approaches to the passages.

Approach I: The Highlighting Technique

This balanced technique is by far the most popular, most common, and most successful.

Passage: 4.5 minutes

Highlighter: Key terms, contrast, opinion, cause-and-effect

Booklet: don't use

Question: 5.5 minutes

With this approach, you will be using the highlighter as your main tool for synthesizing what you're reading. You must **absolutely NOT highlight as you go along**. Instead, stop every 3-4 sentences, ask yourself, "okay what did I just read?" and then select a few words that capture the important ideas you just read. If you just highlight as you read along, you end up with the "paint roller effect" where everything gets highlighted.

Then, when you get to the end of the passage take a moment to ask yourself what the Main Idea was of what you'd just read. Focus on the author's overall opinion and tone. You needn't write it down, but some students find it helpful to do so.

When solving questions, you should be aiming to answer 2-3 of them without looking anything up, and then 2-3 of them may require you to go back and look up facts from the passage. Since you'll have something like 5 minutes to answer the questions, you should have plenty of time do to a bit of "look it up" work.

On the next page you'll find two practice passages. Get a highlighter pen and work through them – don't worry about time for now. Focus on making good choices about what to highlight. Then answer the questions.

After that, you'll see our explanations. There, we have **bold, underlined** text as a way to indicate what's worth highlighting. Compare your choices to our suggestions to see if you missed anything important, or highlighted something that was a minor detail.

Compare your highlighting choices to what came up in the questions – did your highlighting help focus your attention on the things that came up in the questions? If so, great job! If not, you can help your review by going back through the passage with another color of highlighter pen and "fixing" the highlighting so that it's perfect. Then come back and review the passage a week later to remind yourself about what good highlighting looks like.

Highlighting Practice Passage I

Epiphenomenalism is a theory of mind that posits that mental events are caused by underlying physical events, but that those mental events cannot then cause physical changes. That is, it is not the subjective sensation of nervousness that causes perspiration, but rather the perspiration is caused by a physiological reaction. This reaction also produces a sensation of nervousness, but that "feeling" is just a side-effect. Thomas Henry Huxley likened the mind to the whistle on a steam locomotive; while the whistle may announce that the train is coming, it has no effect on the actual operation of the train itself.

The development of epiphenomenalism as a school of thought is rooted in the attempt to solve the basic problem of Cartesian dualism. In the 19th century, philosophers wrestled with the problem of interaction between two seemingly incompatible substances: the mental and the physical. The huge successes of the Enlightenment and the scientific tradition that grew out of it demonstrated humanity's increasing mastery over the realm of the physical, but the mental remained largely opaque, governed by theories and attitudes that could at best be called "folk psychology". In light of this disparity, thinkers in the early 19th century wondered how it was that mind and body could interact.

Descartes posited that there was a special organ – the pineal gland – in the center of the brain that provided a two-way link between the substances of mind and body. This organ explained the truth of our basic perception that the body can affect the mind (e.g. putting wine into the body can cloud the mind), and that the mind can affect the body (e.g. our desire to get some fresh air can send the body out for a walk).

The epiphenomenalists countered that although the mind may be a substance different from the body, it has no causative power on the body. This view flourished as it was consonant with the scientific behaviorism that was coming into vogue at the turn of the 20th century. Such scientific behaviorists, notably Ivan Pavlov, John Watson, and Burrhus Skinner, found great success in their efforts to investigate the relationship between environmental stimuli and behavior exhibited by animals (including humans), while making no reference whatsoever to the mental state of the subject. While such behaviorists would not have made the absurd proposal that the subject has no mental state at all, they simply treated the mental state as causally irrelevant. If an animal's "feelings" cannot have any effect on its behavior, then we may safely ignore them in constructing our experiments and our theories about how animals behave, they held.

Epiphenomenalism faced a number of challenges throughout the past century, but since the cognitive revolution in the 1960's, it has received a number of surprising new avenues of support. In the more modern understanding, mental states are simply physical states in the brain—a thought is simply a pattern of electrical impulses traveling along neurons, a memory a growth of new connections between neurons, a feeling an increased level of certain neurotransmitters in certain anatomical regions. The epiphenomenon is the purely subjective, qualitative aspect of an experience. Such aspects are usually referred to as the "raw feel" of an experience, or the "what-it-is-like", or most often, "qualia". Thus if a dog and a robot that can perfectly mimic the behavior of a dog are both fed a piece of bacon, they will exhibit exactly the same behavior, but only the real dog will be experiencing the qualia of the food. The saltiness of the salt, the richness of the smell, the pleasure of eating will only be present in the epiphenomenal world that is the dog's brain. Both will bark happily, wag their tails, and scarf the food down in a single bite, but only the dog has a mind that will be experiencing the qualia of the food.

A large body of neurophysiological data seem to support epiphenomenalism. Such data includes a number of kinds of electrical potentials which occur in the brain and which cause behavior, and yet happen before the subject is mentally aware of the event. Research shows that it takes at least half a second for a stimulus to become part of conscious experience, and yet subjects are capable of reacting to that stimulus in less than half that time. Thus it is not our consciousness that controls our behavior, but rather our brain reacts and the "mental feeling" of what's happening comes after the fact.

[Adapted from: *Train Whistle in the Head* by Kristen O'Connell-Choate, Tucson Upstairs University Press, 2007]

1. Consider the case of the dog and dog-like robot discussed in the fifth paragraph. Descartes would assert that:
   A) the existence of a robot dog that can perfectly mimic the real dog refutes his theory of dualism.
   B) both the real dog and the robot dog have minds that are linked to their bodies through the pineal gland.
   C) the real dog has a rudimentary mind that is fundamentally different from its body, whereas the robot has only a body.
   D) the robot dog's qualia have some additional, unknowable property that separates the robot dog from the real one.

2. According to the passage, the raw feel of an experience arises from a brain state that is also the cause of any behavior we exhibit

in response to that experience but that the feel itself is causally irrelevant. That view would most be *weakened* if it were discovered that which of the following were true?

A) The electrical potentials that happen in response to a stimulus before the subject is aware of the experience happen most strikingly in the case of olfactory stimuli.

B) When a subject is unconscious they are still capable of reacting to a number of different stimuli.

C) Anger management classes have been shown to stimulate a portion of the prefrontal cortex that is associated with "cooling down" and "thinking things through before you act" and that those regions exhibit activity before subsequent behavioral actions designed to reduce physiological arousal.

D) Meditation techniques that teach a person to avoid harmful repetitive thought patterns have been shown to be effective in the treatment of a number of mental illnesses that had previously only been considered treatable through powerful drugs or surgery.

3. Why does the author discuss the belief of Descartes that the brain has a special gland to mediate interactions between the body and the soul?

A) To show that Descartes's error about the function of the pineal gland serves as a fatal blow to the soundness of his philosophical theory.

B) To refute Descartes's theory of mind/body dualism.

C) To acknowledge that even Descartes knew that true dualism was impossible and that the mind must, at least in part, be a physical thing.

D) To demonstrate that Descartes was aware that physical things that affect the body could alter the mind even though the mind is a fundamentally different substance from the body.

4. The common experience of a violent shocked reaction (shouting, flinching, etc.) when seeing someone in the same room when you thought you were alone, even when that person is someone very familiar serves as evidence:

A) for both epiphenomenalism and materialism.

B) for neither dualism nor epiphenomenalism.

C) for dualism but not epiphenomenalism.

D) against the notion that mind/body interactions are mediated by the pineal gland.

5. Which of the following is most analogous to the function of the mind in epiphenomenalism?

A) The gasoline used to run a motor that drives a boat forward

B) The beauty of a flower that inspires a poet to write a poem

C) The tension an audience feels while watching a suspenseful movie

D) The sunlight glinting off waves on the surface of a calm lake

6. In an experiment subjects are made to look at a series of shocking and disturbing images flashed on the screen for a very short period of time. What does the passage suggest may happen in the brains of these subjects?

A) Their pineal glands will suffer stress in response to the disturbing images.

B) Some physiological responses may occur before the subject is mentally aware of what they're looking at.

C) The parts of their brains responsible for registering disgust will be stimulated only after the subjects have a subjective feeling of disgust.

D) At least some of the subjects will stop looking at the screen after they realize the images are all disturbing.

Highlighting Practice Passage I

Epiphenomenalism is a theory of mind that posits that **mental** events are **caused by underlying physical** events, but that those **mental events cannot then cause physical changes**. That is, it is not the subjective sensation of nervousness that causes perspiration, but rather the perspiration is caused by a physiological reaction. This reaction also produces a sensation of nervousness, but that "**feeling**" is just a **side-effect**. **Thomas Henry Huxley** likened the **mind** to the **whistle on a steam locomotive**; while the whistle may announce that the train is coming, it has **no effect on the actual operation** of the train itself.

Here we've highlighted two technical words – epiphenomenalism and Huxley's name. That's so we can find them again later. We've also highlighted some terms that reveal opinion – the opinion of epiphenomenalism. Remember that opinions can be a school of thought.

The development of epiphenomenalism as a school of thought is rooted in the attempt to **solve** the basic problem of **Cartesian dualism**. In the 19th century, philosophers wrestled with the problem of **interaction** between two **seemingly incompatible** substances: the mental and the physical. The huge successes of the **Enlightenment** and the scientific tradition that grew out of it demonstrated humanity's increasing mastery over the realm of the physical, but the mental remained largely opaque, governed by theories and attitudes that could at best be called "**folk psychology**". In light of this disparity, thinkers in the early 19th century wondered **how it was that mind and body could interact**.

Key terms: Cartesian dualism, Enlightenment, folk psychology

We're given another opinion here – the opinion of philosophers. Highlighting "interaction" "seemingly incompatible" lets us know what they were thinking, "how it was that mind and body could interact".

Descartes posited that there was a special organ – **the pineal gland** – in the center of the brain that provided a **two-way link** between the substances of mind and body. This organ explained the truth of our basic perception that the **body can affect the mind** (e.g. putting wine into the body can cloud the mind), and that the **mind can affect the body** (e.g. our desire to get some fresh air can send the body out for a walk).

Key terms: Descartes, pineal gland

Opinion: Descartes (and thus Cartesian Dualism) asserts that mind can affect physical and physical can affect body.

The epiphenomenalists countered that although the **mind may be a substance different from the body**, it has **no causative power** on the body. This view flourished as it was consonant with the **scientific behaviorism** that was coming into vogue at the turn of the 20th century. Such scientific behaviorists, notably **Ivan Pavlov, John Watson**, and **Burrhus Skinner**, found great success in their efforts to investigate the **relationship between environmental stimuli** and **behavior** exhibited by animals (including humans), while making **no reference whatsoever to the mental state** of the subject. While such behaviorists would **not** have made the absurd proposal that the subject has **no mental state** at all, they simply treated the **mental state as causally irrelevant**. If an animal's "feelings" cannot have any effect on its behavior, then we may safely **ignore** them in constructing our experiments and our theories about how animals behave, they held.

Key terms: behaviorism, Pavlov, Watson, Skinner

Opinion: Behaviorism supports epiphenomenalism by showing you can analyze and predict behavior with no reference to mental states (not that they don't exist, but they don't matter)

Epiphenomenalism faced a number of **challenges** throughout the past century, but since the **cognitive revolution in the 1960's**, it has received a number of **surprising new avenues of support**. In the more modern understanding, **mental** states are simply **physical states in the brain**—a thought is simply a pattern of electrical impulses traveling along neurons, a memory a growth of new connections between neurons, a feeling an increased level of certain neurotransmitters in certain anatomical regions. The **epiphenomenon** is the **purely subjective, qualitative aspect** of an experience. Such aspects are usually referred to as the "**raw feel**" of an experience, or the "what-it-is-like", or most often, "**qualia**". Thus if a dog and a robot that can perfectly mimic the behavior of a dog are both fed a piece of bacon, they will exhibit exactly the same behavior, but **only the real dog** will be experiencing the **qualia** of the food. The saltiness of the salt, the richness of the smell, the pleasure of eating will only be present in the epiphenomenal world that is the dog's brain. Both will bark happily, wag their tails, and scarf the food down in a single bite, but only the dog has a mind that will be experiencing the qualia of the food.

Key terms: cognitive revolution, raw feel, qualia

Opinion: After the cognitive revolution we've come to see mental states as just physical states in the brain.

Contrast: A robot dog that exactly mimics a real dog could reproduce all of the behaviors but wouldn't experience the qualia the way the dog does.

A large body of **neurophysiological data** seem to **support epiphenomenalism**. Such data includes a number of kinds of **electrical potentials** which occur in the brain and which cause behavior, and yet **happen before the subject is mentally aware** of the event. Research shows that it takes at least half a second for a stimulus to become part of conscious experience, and yet subjects are **capable of reacting to that stimulus in less than half that time**. Thus it is not our consciousness that controls our behavior, but rather our brain reacts and the "**mental feeling**" of what's happening **comes after** the fact.

[Adapted from: *Train Whistle in the Head* by Kristen O'Connell-Choate, Tucson Upstairs University Press, 2007]

Key terms: neurophysiological data, mental feeling

Cause-and-effect: New data show that the brain is capable of reacting to things faster than the person is capable of becoming consciously aware. Thus the conscious awareness is not the thing causing the physical reaction.

Main Idea: Epiphenomenalism contrasts with dualism by saying that physical can affect mental but that mental has no control over physical. Support for epiphenomenalism has come from behaviorism, the cognitive revolution, and neurophysiology.

Remember, on test day you don't necessarily have to stop and write out the Main Idea. What you do need to do is stop, take a moment to gather your thoughts – look over all of your highlighting, essentially re-skimming the passage just looking to your highlights. In doing so, formulate the Main Idea in your mind.

1. Consider the case of the dog and dog-like robot discussed in the fifth paragraph. Descartes would assert that:
A) the existence of a robot dog that can perfectly mimic the real dog refutes his theory of dualism.
B) both the real dog and the robot dog have minds that are linked to their bodies through the pineal gland.
C) the real dog has a rudimentary mind that is fundamentally different from its body, whereas the robot has only a body.
D) the robot dog's qualia have some additional, unknowable property that separates the robot dog from the real one.

Descartes thinks that mind and body are two fundamentally different things, but that they can have a causal relationship with each other through the pineal gland. Descartes would certainly not think that a robot dog had a mind or qualia of any kind. Thus choice C is correct.

2. According to the passage, the raw feel of an experience arises from a brain state that is also the cause of any behavior we exhibit in response to that experience but that the feel itself is causally irrelevant. That view would most be *weakened* if it were discovered that which of the following were true?

A) The electrical potentials that happen in response to a stimulus before the subject is aware of the experience happen most strikingly in the case of olfactory stimuli.

B) When a subject is unconscious they are still capable of reacting to a number of different stimuli.

C) Anger management classes have been shown to stimulate a portion of the prefrontal cortex that is associated with "cooling down" and "thinking things through before you act" and that those regions exhibit activity before subsequent behavioral actions designed to reduce physiological arousal.

D) Meditation techniques that teach a person to avoid harmful repetitive thought patterns have been shown to be effective in the treatment of a number of mental illnesses that had previously only been considered treatable through powerful drugs or surgery.

To refute epiphenomenalism we need a case where someone can mentally think something through (have a conscious experience of thinking something over) and that is able to then cause physical responses. In the case of choice C, the person is able to think things through before activating the physiological response that lets them calm down. Thus C is the correct answer because it suggests that the conscious experience of thinking things through comes before and leads to the actual physiological calming down.

3. Why does the author discuss the belief of Descartes that the brain has a special gland to mediate interactions between the body and the soul?

A) To show that Descartes's error about the function of the pineal gland serves as a fatal blow to the soundness of his philosophical theory.

B) To refute Descartes's theory of mind/body dualism.

C) To acknowledge that even Descartes knew that true dualism was impossible and that the mind must, at least in part, be a physical thing.

D) To demonstrate that Descartes was aware that physical things that affect the body could alter the mind even though the mind is a fundamentally different substance from the body.

Descartes believed that mind and body could interact with each other somehow – that mind could cause physical changes and that physical changes (like drinking alcohol) could affect the mind. If mind and body are two very different things, we're left wondering how they could interact. So the author tells us Descartes' answer: the brain had a special organ (the pineal gland) to achieve that end. Thus choice D is correct.

4. The common experience of a violent shocked reaction (shouting, flinching, etc.) when seeing someone in the same room when you thought you were alone, even when that person is someone very familiar serves as evidence:

A) for both epiphenomenalism and materialism.

B) for neither dualism nor epiphenomenalism.

C) for dualism but not epiphenomenalism.

D) against the notion that mind/body interactions are mediated by the pineal gland.

The argument about dualism and epiphenomenalism rests on causality: can the mind cause physical changes or not? Dualism says yes, epiphenomenalism says no. Shouting in surprise does not, in itself, address the question. Thus choice B is correct. For the situation in the question to be relevant we would have to be told something about the causal links – did the person shout before experiencing surprise, or have the feeling of surprise and then shout in response.

5. Which of the following is most analogous to the function of the mind in epiphenomenalism?

A) The gasoline used to run a motor that drives a boat forward

B) The beauty of a flower that inspires a poet to write a poem

C) The tension an audience feels while watching a suspenseful movie

D) The sunlight glinting off waves on the surface of a calm lake

The example in the passage says that the mind is like the whistle on a train: related to the arrival of the train, but not with any causal power over the train itself. So we need something where the epiphenomenon has no ability to cause the underlying phenomenon. Choice D is the best fit – the glint of sunlight is caused by the small ripples in the water's surface, but the glinting doesn't cause (and can't cause) the underlying waves.

6. In an experiment subjects are made to look at a series of shocking and disturbing images flashed on the screen for a very short period of time. What does the passage suggest may happen in the brains of these subjects?

A) Their pineal glands will suffer stress in response to the disturbing images.

B) Some physiological responses may occur before the subject is mentally aware of what they're looking at.

C) The parts of their brains responsible for registering disgust will be stimulated only after the subjects have a subjective feeling of disgust.

D) At least some of the subjects will stop looking at the screen after they realize the images are all disturbing.

The final paragraph tells us that some neurophysiology studies have shown that people's brains are capable of reacting faster than the person actually becomes aware of something. That matches choice B.

Highlighting Practice Passage II

The needs that are usually taken as the starting point for motivation theory are the so-called physiological drives. Two recent lines of research make it necessary to revise our customary notions about these needs, first, the development of the concept of homeostasis, and second, the finding that appetites (preferential choices among foods) are a fairly efficient indication of actual needs or lacks in the body.

Thus it seems impossible as well as useless to make any list of fundamental physiological needs for they can come to almost any number one might wish, depending on the degree of specificity of description. We cannot identify all physiological needs as homeostatic. That sexual desire, sleepiness, sheer activity and maternal behavior in animals, are homeostatic has not yet been demonstrated. Furthermore, this list would not include the various sensory pleasures (tastes, smells, tickling, stroking) which are probably physiological and which may become the goals of motivated behavior.

In a previous paper it has been pointed out that these physiological drives or needs are to be considered unusual rather than typical because they are isolable, and because they are localizable somatically. That is to say, they are relatively independent of each other, of other motivations and of the organism as a whole, and secondly, in many cases, it is possible to demonstrate a localized, underlying somatic base for the drive. This is true less generally than has been thought (exceptions are fatigue, sleepiness, maternal responses) but it is still true in the classic instances of hunger, sex, and thirst.

It should be pointed out again that any of the physiological needs and the consummatory behavior involved with them serve as channels for all sorts of other needs as well. That is to say, the person who thinks he is hungry may actually be seeking more for comfort, or dependence, than for vitamins or proteins. Conversely, it is possible to satisfy the hunger need in part by other activities such as drinking water or smoking cigarettes. In other words, relatively isolable as these physiological needs are, they are not completely so.

Undoubtedly these physiological needs are the most pre-potent of all needs. What this means specifically is, that in the human being who is missing everything in life in an extreme fashion, it is most likely that the major motivation would be the physiological needs rather than any others. A person who is lacking food, safety, love, and esteem would most probably hunger for food more strongly than for anything else.

[Adapted from "A Theory of Human Motivation", *Psychological Review*, by A.H. Maslow, 1943.]

1. The author would probably agree with which of the following statements about physiological drives?

A) A few of the fundamental physiological needs still need to be identified.

B) Homeostasis is the result of satisfying a physiological need.

C) The physiological drives do not form a discrete, clearly-defined category.

D) The strongest physiological drives refer to those needs which are socially-oriented.

2. What is the author's purpose in writing, in the final paragraph, that food would take precedence over the other needs listed?

A) To support his argument that urgency and priority are a better definition of physiological needs than homeostasis.

B) To argue that hunger is a fundamental physiological drive, while love and safety aren't.

C) To show an example of the non-isolable nature of even the fundamental physiological needs.

D) To prove that fundamental physiological needs cannot be met by alternate activities.

3. An energy-dense drink like soda often meets energy needs far before it provides the person consuming it with a sense of fullness. The passage author would probably consider this:

A) an example of the overlapping nature of some physiological needs.

B) evidence of the non-physiological nature of hunger.

C) evidence that social training can overcome or confuse physiological drives.

D) an indication that hunger is non-homeostatic.

4. What is the author's purpose in writing, in the second paragraph, that not all physiological needs have been confirmed to be homeostatic?

A) To support the inclusion of sensory pleasures to the list of recognized physiological needs.

B) To introduce the unconfirmed needs, sexual desire, sleepiness, maternal instinct, etc.

C) To provide further evidence against homeostasis as a dominant organizing principle.

D) To provide evidence that the present definition of physiological needs is problematic.

5. Biologist Ernst Mayr argued that complex biological phenomena generally could not always be broken down to sets of simple, isolated relationships, but would remain intertwined and mathematically inexact. The passage author would likely

A) agree that biological reductionism is a dead end.

B) admit that perfect isolability is impossible.

C) acknowledge the difficulty in reductionism, but not its irrelevance.

D) dismiss the idea that a simple, rule-based understanding can never be achieved.

Highlighting Practice Passage II

The needs that are usually taken as the starting point for **motivation theory** are the so-called **physiological drives**. Two recent lines of research make it necessary to revise our customary notions about these needs, first, the development of the concept of **homeostasis**, and second, the finding that **appetites** (preferential choices among foods) are a fairly efficient **indication of actual needs** or lacks in the body.

Key terms: motivation theory, physiological drives, homeostasis

Cause-and-effect: knowledge of homeostasis and the relation between appetites and bodily needs both affect prior understanding of drives

Thus it seems **impossible** as well as useless to make any **list of fundamental physiological needs** for they can come to almost any number one might wish, depending on the degree of specificity of description. **We cannot identify all physiological needs as homeostatic**. That sexual desire, sleepiness, sheer activity and maternal behavior in animals, **are homeostatic, has not yet been demonstrated**. Furthermore, this list would not include the **various sensory pleasures** (tastes, smells, tickling, stroking) which are probably physiological and which may become the goals of motivated behavior.

Contrast: some physiological needs are homeostatic, some may not be, some definitely aren't

Cause-and-effect: the way in which needs are defined determines which can be thus classified

Opinion: an unobjective, uncertain classification has no use

In a previous paper it has been pointed out that these physiological drives or needs are to be considered **unusual rather than typical** because they are **isolable**, and because they are **localizable somatically**. That is to say, they are relatively independent of each other, of other motivations and of the organism as a whole, and secondly, in many cases, it is possible to demonstrate a **localized, underlying somatic base** for the drive. This is true less generally than has been thought (exceptions are fatigue, sleepiness, maternal responses) but it is still true in the **classic instances of hunger, sex, and thirst**.

Key terms: isolable, localizable

Contrast: previously isolability and localizability were considered defining characteristics, now considered exceptional

Cause-and-effect: a clear location and physiological cause define classic, well-understood drives

It should be pointed out again that any of the physiological needs and the **consummatory behavior** involved with them serve as **channels for all sorts of other needs** as well. That is to say, the person who **thinks he is hungry** may actually be seeking more for comfort, or dependence, than for vitamins or proteins. Conversely, it is possible to **satisfy the hunger** need in part **by other activities** such as drinking water or smoking cigarettes. In other words, **relatively isolable** as these physiological needs are, they are not completely so.

Key terms: consummatory behavior

Contrast: traditional consummatory behavior, a need arises from a biological imperative, leading to behavior that satisfies the underlying cause (dehydration causes thirst causes rehydration through drinking), but other causes and consummations can be the cause or result of this need

Cause-and-effect: other needs (than need of food) may cause hunger, other responses (than eating) may satisfy hunger

Undoubtedly these physiological needs are the most **pre-potent** of all needs. What this means specifically is, that in the human being who is missing everything in life in an extreme fashion, it is most likely that the **major motivation** would be the **physiological needs** rather than any others. A person who is lacking food, safety, love, and esteem would most probably hunger for food more strongly than for anything else.

[Adapted from "A Theory of Human Motivation", *Psychological Review*, by A.H. Maslow, 1943.]

Key terms: pre-potent

Contrast: hunger is pre-potent and takes precedence, love and safety are secondary

Cause-and-effect: of several needs, physiological needs (being pre-potent) are strongest, take precedence in consummatory behavior

Main Idea: Homeostasis doesn't fully explain even physiological needs as motivators and what may seem like fundamental physiological needs can't fully be isolated, since they may be expressions of emotional needs, or may be satisfied by other behaviors.

1. The author would probably agree with which of the following statements about physiological drives?

   A) A few of the fundamental physiological needs still need to be identified.

   B) Homeostasis is the result of satisfying a physiological need.

   C) The physiological drives do not form a discrete, clearly-defined category.

   D) The strongest physiological drives refer to those needs which are socially-oriented.

The passage describes the current difficulties in clearly categorizing physiological drives, citing their imperfect isolability as a major issue.

A: This is not supported by the passage.

B: This contradicts the passage, which cites several needs that are not homeostatic in nature.

D: This contradicts the passage, which states that hunger would override drives involving other people, such as love or esteem.

2. What is the author's purpose in writing, in the final paragraph, that food would take precedence over the other needs listed?

A) To support his argument that urgency and priority are a better definition of physiological needs than homeostasis.

B) To argue that hunger is a fundamental physiological drive, while love and safety aren't.

C) To show an example of the non-isolable nature of even the fundamental physiological needs.

D) To prove that fundamental physiological needs cannot be met by alternate activities.

Throughout the passage, the author has been arguing about the difficult in recognizing and categorizing different drives/needs. He shows the problem with homeostasis as a defining factor. In the last paragraph, he returns to some of the currently acknowledged needs, but alights on their pre-potency, demonstrating the urgency to satisfy these needs, and the way they take priority over other needs. The implication is that this definition works where others have failed.

B: This may be true, but the author seems to have assumed from the start that hunger, one of the classic drives, is physiological. The question at hand was, why is this so?

C: This paragraph had nothing to do with isolability.

D: This is contradicted elsewhere in the passage and irrelevant to the section being discussed.

3. An energy-dense drink like soda often meets energy needs far before it provides the person consuming it with a sense of fullness. The passage author would probably consider this

A) an example of the overlapping nature of some physiological needs.

B) evidence of the non-physiological nature of hunger.

C) evidence that social training can overcome or confuse physiological drives.

D) an indication that hunger is non-homeostatic.

The statement in this question stem suggests that, despite hunger being a drive leading to the ingestion of food, the need can be met, at least from a caloric perspective, without curtailing the hunger itself. This is similar to another example given in the passage, where something with no calories can satisfy hunger, given enough of it, and likewise suggests that needs are not perfectly isolable. A is a match.

B: The physiological nature of hunger is not at question in this passage.

C: Nothing like this is discussed in the passage.

D: That the hunger drive can be fooled does not necessarily mean it is not homeostatic, and, again, were this evidence, it's not an argument the passage author had made about hunger.

4. What is the author's purpose in writing, in the second paragraph, that not all physiological needs have been confirmed to be homeostatic?

A) To support the inclusion of sensory pleasures to the list of recognized physiological needs.

B) To introduce the unconfirmed needs, sexual desire, sleepiness, maternal instinct, etc.

C) To provide further evidence against homeostasis as a dominant organizing principle.

D) To provide evidence that the present definition of physiological needs is problematic.

The entire passage is devoted to sussing out the difficulties in identifying the physiological needs, given several contradictory definitions, none of which work for each need traditionally listed. That paragraph is devoted to the issues with the homeostatic definition, but is still in service to that larger goal. D is thus a match.

A: This answer choice switches evidence and conclusion. The sensory pleasures were cited as another problem with the homeostatic definition; the passage author took it as a given that they were physiological in nature.

B: These were clearly only included as examples to support the claim that many needs are not homeostatic, not the main purpose of the paragraph.

C: The passage author does not attack homeostasis itself, which explains many bodily processes, merely the definition of physiological needs as homeostatically-motivated.

5. Biologist Ernst Mayr argued that complex biological phenomena generally could not always be broken down to sets of simple, isolated relationships, but would remain intertwined and mathematically inexact. The passage author would likely

A) agree that biological reductionism is a dead end.

B) admit that perfect isolability is impossible.

C) acknowledge the difficulty in reductionism, but not its irrelevance.

D) dismiss the idea that a simple, rule-based understanding can never be achieved.

The passage suggests that the non-isolability of many physiological needs is, in fact, a problem, making it more difficult to understand the drives they feed. At the end, the passage author suggests a new definition, based on a simple hierarchy, to classify physiological and non-physiological needs. C is the best match for this.

A: This is not supported by the passage.

B: Though not all needs are isolable, it seems to be assumed that some biological processes are.

D: Too extreme. Reductionism may be desirable, but the passage acknowledges the difficulty.

Approach II: The Note-taking Technique

This slow-read technique is the most common taught in big lecture courses offered by prep companies. It's also one of the least popular among students. The mistake here is that students feel like the note-taking slows them down. They try it once, conclude that they don't like, and just throw out the whole enterprise.

This is a major mistake – for many students a slow, careful read with judicious note-taking can be very valuable. The key here isn't to write down lots and lots of notes – you wouldn't, for example, write down nearly as many words as you'd highlight when using the highlighting technique.

Instead, the key aspect of the note-taking technique is that you're giving the passage a very thorough, very careful read. The note-taking is simply a way to get you to slow down and focus very precisely on what you're reading. Then, when going through the questions move fast and never look anything up.

Passage: 6 – 6.5 to 7 minutes

Highlighter: only proper nouns, if any

Booklet: notes after each paragraph

Question: 3 – 3.5 minutes

Finally, at the end of the passage, ***write down the main idea***. You need to formulate the main idea thoroughly and precisely and get it on paper. Since you're not going to be looking things up in the passage, having the main idea down on paper is a valuable tool.

Ironically, the slow-read approach often works best for students who are very strong readers and are comfortable reading very quickly. Typically students who spent a lot of time reading in college – English majors, Philosophy majors, etc. – are the ones that find the most success with this approach.

Because students who are fast readers can move through the sentences very quickly, they can afford to read each sentence or paragraph two (or even three) times to really master what it says.

Again, don't dismiss this approach immediately. Give it plenty of practice to decide if you find it helpful. If, after doing the two practice passages here, the half-section and the full section that are allocated for note-taking practice, you find you still can't make it work and don't like it, then by all means set this approach aside.

Note-taking Practice Passage I

The mere physical vision of the poet may or may not be any keener than the vision of other men. There is an infinite variety in the bodily endowments of habitual verse-makers: there have been near-sighted poets like Tennyson, far-sighted poets like Wordsworth, and, in the well-known case of Robert Browning, a poet conveniently far-sighted in one eye and near-sighted in the other! No doubt the life-long practice of observing and recording natural phenomena sharpens the sense of poets, as it does the senses of Indians, naturalists, sailors and all outdoors men. The quick eye for costume and character possessed by a Chaucer or a Shakespeare is remarkable, but equally so is the observation of a Dickens or a Balzac. It is rather in what we call psychical vision that the poet is wont to excel, that is, in his ability to perceive the meaning of visual phenomena. Here he ceases to be a mere reporter of retinal images, and takes upon himself the higher and harder function of an interpreter of the visible world. He has no immunity from the universal human experiences: he loves and he is angry and he sees men born and die. He becomes according to the measure of his intellectual capacity a thinker. He strives to see into the human heart, to comprehend the working of the human mind. He reads the divine justice in the tragic fall of Kings. He penetrates beneath the external forms of Nature and perceives her as a "living presence." Yet the faculty of vision, which the poet possesses in so eminent a degree, is shared by many who are not poets. Darwin's outward eye was as keen as Wordsworth's; St. Paul's sense of the reality of the invisible world is more wonderful than Shakespeare's. The poet is indeed first of all a seer, but he must be something more than a seer before he is wholly poet.

Another mark of the poetic mind is its vivid sense of relations. The part suggests the whole. In the single instance there is a hint of the general law. The self-same Power that brings the fresh rhodora to the woods brings the poet there also. In the field-mouse, the daisy, the water-fowl, he beholds types and symbols. His own experience stands for all men's. The conscience-stricken Macbeth is a poet when he cries, "Life is a walking shadow," and King Lear makes the same pathetic generalization when he exclaims, "What, have his daughters brought him to this pass?" Through the shifting phenomena of the present the poet feels the sweep of the universe; his mimic play and "the great globe itself" are alike an "insubstantial pageant," though it may happen, as Tennyson said of Wordsworth, that even in the transient he gives the sense of the abiding, "whose dwelling is the light of setting suns." But this perception of relations, characteristic as it is of the poetic temper, is also an attribute of the philosopher. The intellect of a Newton, too, leaps from the specific instance to the general law.

The real difference between "the poet" and other men is … in his capacity for making and employing verbal images of a certain kind, and combining these images into rhythmical and metrical designs. In each of his functions—as "seer," as "maker," and as "singer"—he shows himself a true creator. Criticism no longer attempts to act as his "law-giver," to assert what he may or may not do. The poet is free, like every creative artist, to make a beautiful object in any way he can. And nevertheless criticism—watching countless poets lovingly for many a century, observing their various endowments, their manifest endeavors, their victories and defeats, observing likewise the nature of language, that strange medium (so much stranger than any clay or bronze!) through which poets are compelled to express their conceptions—criticism believes that poetry, like each of the sister arts, has its natural province, its own field of the beautiful. ... In W. H. Hudson's Green Mansions the reader will remember how a few sticks and stones, laid upon a hilltop, were used as markers to indicate the outlines of a continent. Criticism, likewise, needs its poor sticks and stones of commonplace, if it is to point out any roadway. Our own road leads first into the difficult territory of the poet's imaginings, and then into the more familiar world of the poet's words.

[Adapted from *A Study of Poetry*, Chapter II. Bliss Perry, 1920.]

1. The passage asserts that the uniqueness of the poet stems from his:

I. habit of separating himself physically from the drudgery and commonality of day-to-day experience.

II. acute sense of the immediate as an entity removed from the confounding filter of human interpretation.

III. ability to reshape verbal imagery according to a specific design.

A) I only   B) III only
C) I and III only   D) II and III only

2. Throughout the passage, the author advances his primary argument by comparing and contrasting:

A) the poet and his poetry.

B) false vision and real experience.

C) poets and other artists and thinkers.

D) the subtlety and palpability of poetry.

3. If this passage were included with other pieces of writing on poetry containing central themes consistent with that of this passage, writings with which of the following themes would be most appropriate to include?

A) Modern native poets

B) Universal techniques of poetic analysis

C) That which typifies the poetical

D) A critical belief that the parallels between poetry and other fine arts threaten the uniqueness of its literary province

4. The sentence "It is rather in what we call psychical vision that the poet is wont to excel, that is, in his ability to perceive the meaning of visual phenomena," in the first paragraph is most probably included by the author in order to:

A) define the distinct provenance of the poet by offering a descriptive insight into his interpretive process.

B) highlight the poet's great difficulty in transcending the limitations of immediate vision in their writing.

C) emphasize the poet's exclusive role as a seer.

D) underscore the uniqueness of the poet's capacity for interpreting the meaning of that which he sees.

5. The author seems to suggest that a reader's appreciation of a poet's work stems from:

A) the need to separate out the elements of poetry born from the poet's multiple roles as seer, marker and singer.

B) the difficulty of navigating the literal meaning of a poet's work.

C) the need to transcend the barrier of dissimilar experience between reader and poet.

D) the reader finding insight in the mind of a poet.

6. Based upon the passage text, the author most probably finds the role of the critic in relation to the poet to be one of:

A) imposing strict limitations on the work poets may produce.

B) interpreting the common elements of poets' work.

C) liaison, bridging the gap between reader and poet.

D) judge, putting forth a positive or negative assessment of the absolute merit of poetic works.

7. In the final sentence of the second paragraph, the author makes reference to "The intellect of Newton," in order to:

A) provide an example illustrating a preceding assertion qualifying an element of the poetic temper.

B) emphasize his claim that the scientific mind operates differently than that of the poet.

C) support his assertion that a vivid sense of relation, shared by the philosopher, is necessary and sufficient to define the poetic mind.

D) strengthen his description of the role of the poet as a thinker according to his "intellectual capacity".

Note-taking Practice Passage I

The mere physical vision of the poet may or may not be any keener than the vision of other men. There is an infinite variety in the bodily endowments of habitual verse-makers: there have been near-sighted poets like **Tennyson**, far-sighted poets like **Wordsworth**, and, in the well-known case of Robert **Browning**, a poet conveniently far-sighted in one eye and near-sighted in the other! No doubt the life-long practice of observing and recording natural phenomena sharpens the sense of poets, as it does the senses of Indians, naturalists, sailors and all outdoors men. The quick eye for costume and character possessed by a **Chaucer** or a **Shakespeare** is remarkable, but equally so is the observation of a **Dickens** or a **Balzac**. It is rather in what we call psychical vision that the poet is wont to excel, that is, in his ability to perceive the meaning of visual phenomena. Here he ceases to be a mere reporter of retinal images, and takes upon himself the higher and harder function of an interpreter of the visible world. He has no immunity from the universal human experiences: he loves and he is angry and he sees men born and die. He becomes according to the measure of his intellectual capacity a thinker. He strives to see into the human heart, to comprehend the working of the human mind. He reads the divine justice in the tragic fall of Kings. He penetrates beneath the external forms of Nature and perceives her as a "living presence." Yet the faculty of vision, which the poet possesses in so eminent a degree, is shared by many who are not poets. **Darwin's** outward eye was as keen as Wordsworth's; St. Paul's sense of the reality of the invisible world is more wonderful than Shakespeare's. The poet is indeed first of all a seer, but he must be something more than a seer before he is wholly poet.

Scratch Notes: Auth thinks poets are different from other men in their psychical vision, true poet = seer but more than that.

Another mark of the poetic mind is its vivid sense of relations. The part suggests the whole. In the single instance there is a hint of the general law. The self-same Power that brings the fresh rhodora to the woods brings the poet there also. In the field-mouse, the daisy, the water-fowl, he beholds types and symbols. His own experience stands for all men's. The conscience-stricken **Macbeth** is a poet when he cries, "Life is a walking shadow," and **King Lear** makes the same pathetic generalization when he exclaims, "What, have his daughters brought him to this pass?" Through the shifting phenomena of the present the poet feels the sweep of the universe; his mimic play and "the great globe itself" are alike an "insubstantial pageant," though it may happen, as Tennyson said of Wordsworth, that even in the transient he gives the sense of the abiding, "whose dwelling is the light of setting suns." But this perception of relations, characteristic as it is of the poetic temper, is also an attribute of the philosopher. The intellect of a Newton, too, leaps from the specific instance to the general law.

Scratch Notes: Poet must be seer + able think in univ. + general. Facility for the univ. also in philos + sci

The real difference between "the poet" and other men is … in his capacity for making and employing verbal images of a certain kind, and combining these images into rhythmical and metrical designs. In each of his functions–as "seer," as "maker," and as "singer"–he shows himself a true creator. Criticism no longer attempts to act as his "law-giver," to assert what he may or may not do. The poet is free, like every creative artist, to make a beautiful object in any way he can. And nevertheless criticism–watching countless poets lovingly for many a century, observing their various endowments, their manifest endeavors, their victories and defeats, observing likewise the nature of language, that strange medium (so much stranger than any clay or bronze!) through which poets are compelled to express their conceptions–criticism believes that poetry, like each of the sister arts, has its natural province, its own field of the beautiful. … In **W. H. Hudson's Green Mansions** the reader will remember how a few sticks and stones, laid upon a hilltop, were used as markers to indicate the outlines of a continent. Criticism, likewise, needs its poor sticks and stones of commonplace, if it is to point out any roadway. Our own road leads first into the difficult territory of the poet's imaginings, and then into the more familiar world of the poet's words.

[Adapted from *A Study of Poetry*, Chapter II. Bliss Perry, 1920.]

Scratch Notes: What sep. poet from other = verbal images in metrical designs, criticism believe poetry beautiful and crit. has own tools to look at poet's imaginings and words.

Main Idea: A poet must have a keen insight into the world, possess an ability to see the universal underlying the particular, and have a unique ability to craft verbal images in a rhythmical pattern. Critics of poetry recognize its beauty and use their own "sticks and stones" to appreciate it.

1. The passage asserts that the uniqueness of the poet stems from his:

I. habit of separating himself physically from the drudgery and commonality of day-to-day experience.

II. acute sense of the immediate as an entity removed from the confounding filter of human interpretation.

III. ability to reshape verbal imagery according to a specific design.

A) I only

B) III only

C) I and III only

D) II and III only

I: False. The passage explicitly states in the first paragraph that the poet "has no immunity from the universal human experience."

II: False. The second paragraph in particular describes the poet's work as having a vivid sense of the relations [between things], of finding a hint of the general in specific instances and, in the second paragraph, as having a "sense of the abiding" and of the "sweep of the universe." Taken together, the author suggests that the poet does not have a strictly isolated sense of the immediate, but that he interprets and relates events by way of his human experience. But, in any case, this statement is incorrect because, from the end of the second paragraph, "this perception of relations, characteristic as it is of the poetic temper, is an also an attribute of the philosopher" and is not, as the question asks, something that is unique to the poet.

III: True. The passage explains in the last paragraph that "the real difference between "the poet" and other men is … in his capacity for making and employing verbal imagery … combining these images into rhythmical and metrical designs."

2. Throughout the passage, the author advances his primary argument by comparing and contrasting:

A) the poet and his poetry.

B) false vision and real experience.

C) poets and other artists and thinkers.

D) the subtlety and palpability of poetry.

The main thrust of the passage is describing the common habits of poets and how they are similar or dissimilar to those of other thinkers and artists in support of the passage's main goal of defining what makes a poet unique.

A: The author never directly compares or contrasts poets with their individual works.

B: While the passage does explore the nature of a poet's vision, the author explains the process in terms of expanding and interpreting experiences and relationships. He doesn't suggest that any "vision" is less real than "experience."

D: While the subtlety and palpability of poetry may be referred to obliquely as elements of different poets' works in the first and second paragraphs, it's not a continued or central theme of the poet. That main theme is, instead, explaining, as the first sentence of the third paragraph says, "the real difference between 'the poet' and other men."

3. If this passage were included with other pieces of writing on poetry containing central themes consistent with that of this passage, writings with which of the following themes would be most appropriate to include?

A) Modern native poets

B) Universal techniques of poetic analysis

C) That which typifies the poetical

D) A critical belief that the parallels between poetry and other fine arts threaten the uniqueness of its literary province

The passage seeks out and explains those things that are both common and unique to the poet in the process of writing; such an exposition would fit well in a more general discussion of what defines poetry.

A: The passage includes examples of poets from different time periods and places, not just modern or native poets. The passage's central theme is what universally makes poets unique from other artists, and doesn't focus on sub-groups of poets.

B: While the passage does touch on poetic analysis when discussing the place of criticism, it's less central to the passage than the main theme of what uniquely defines poets.

D: This choice implies that drawing parallels between poetry and other art threatens poetry's place as a separate art form. The third paragraph specifically claims agreement among critics that poetry does occupy its own space in the realm of fine arts contradicting the choice and meaning that any effort to draw parallels between poetry and other art forms would pose no threat to poetry's place.

4. The sentence "It is rather in what we call psychical vision that the poet is wont to excel, that is, in his ability to perceive the meaning of visual phenomena," in the first paragraph is most probably included by the author in order to:

A) define the distinct provenance of the poet by offering a descriptive insight into his interpretive process.

B) highlight the poet's great difficulty in transcending the limitations of immediate vision in their writing.

C) emphasize the poet's exclusive role as a seer

D) underscore the uniqueness of the poet's capacity for interpreting the meaning of that which he sees.

The sentence gives context to the first paragraph's concluding claim that the poet acts importantly as a seer, by explaining and emphasizing the poet's ability to see psychically (through interpretation in their mind's eye) visual phenomena.

B: This is precisely the opposite of what the sentence claims; according to the sentence, and in keeping with the passage, the poet is adept at transcending the limitations of physical vision and interpreting the implications of both the seen and unseen. Be careful to correctly interpret the use of the word "wont" in the sentence, by keeping in mind the logical progression of the passage.

C: While the final sentence of the first paragraph does state that the poet must first act as a seer, it continues on to say that "... he must be something more than a seer before he is wholly poet." Acting as a seer then, being a "mere reporter of retinal images" as the first paragraph describes it, is a common function performed by many, not by poets exclusively.

D: This is directly contradicted by the passage's claim that the poet's "faculty of vision ... is shared by many who are not poets."

5. The author seems to suggest that a reader's appreciation of a poet's work stems from:

A) the need to separate out the elements of poetry born from the poet's multiple roles as seer, marker and singer.

B) the difficulty of navigating the literal meaning of a poet's work.

C) the need to transcend the barrier of dissimilar experience between reader and poet.

D) the reader finding insight in the mind of a poet.

In the final paragraph, the passage is fairly explicit about the role of the reader: to understand the imaginings of the poet. The last sentence of the last paragraph concludes that the "[reader's] road leads first into the difficult territory of the poet's imaginings" and only then into the easier and "more familiar world of the poet's words."

A: While the last paragraph does describe the multiple roles played by the poet, it's not suggested that tension exists in satisfying those roles, or that evidence of multiple roles is apparent in poets' work.

B: The last sentence of the passage states that understanding the poet's words is easier than placing those words in context of the "poet's imaginings."

C: While this may or may not be true in real life, the passage doesn't make reference to it. This choice is out of scope.

6. Based upon the passage text, the author most probably finds the role of the critic in relation to the poet to be one of:

A) imposing strict limitations on the work poets may produce.

B) interpreting the common elements of poets' work.

C) liaison, bridging the gap between reader and poet.

D) judge, putting forth a positive or negative assessment of the absolute merit of poetic works.

Answering this question correctly requires an understanding of the critic's role as described in the passage. In keeping with the larger goal being described in this passage—finding those things uniquely common to poets in accomplishing their work—the last paragraph describes how critics can act in this capacity to outline the creative paths followed by poets.

A: The final paragraph suggests that while critics in the past may have acted, or attempted to act, in this manner, they no longer do.

C: The author describes the critic and reader as facing similar challenges, but as having different tasks, as the reader must follow "…[his] own road."

D: This may be a tempting response but such a role for a literary critic isn't what's being specifically described in the passage. Instead, the passage conceives of the critic as one who seeks to understand the nature and dimensions of poetry.

7. In the final sentence of the second paragraph, the author makes reference to "The intellect of Newton," in order to:

A) provide an example illustrating a preceding assertion qualifying an element of the poetic temper.

B) emphasize his claim that the scientific mind operates differently than that of the poet.

C) support his assertion that a vivid sense of relation, shared by the philosopher, is necessary and sufficient to define the poetic mind.

D) strengthen his description of the role of the poet as a thinker according to his "intellectual capacity".

This question asks about the author's intent. Pay close attention to the preceding sentences describing poets' minds moving from specific instances to the general. This is the same as the description of Newton's intellect in the reference sentence. The passage refers to Newton (as an example of another thinker who generalizes from specific examples in the course of a creative process) in order to support the passage's claim that generalization is a quality common to, but not unique to, poets. If Newton, a scientist, generalized from the specific, then, while generalization is held to be an important characteristic of the poet as highlighted by the examples of generalizing poets in the second paragraph, then it can't be unique to the poet. The inclusion of Newton then serves to make the point that generalization is not exclusive to the poetic mind.

B: No such claim is made. In fact, this sentence draws a parallel between the functioning of the poetic and scientific mind; both the poet and scientist, as represented by Newton, infer the general from specific instances.

C: The vivid sense of relation referred to in the opening sentence of the second paragraph is "characteristic" of a poet, but not alone sufficient to define the poetic mind, as others share the characteristic.

D: In spite of the common use of the word "intellect" in both lines, the reference to Newton's intellect isn't included in order to draw a comparison to the role of the poet as a thinker, but rather to act as a specific example of Newton as a generalizing thinker.

Note-taking Practice Passage II

Bright young scientists must learn through trial-and-error to separate failure to achieve the expected results from failure of the experiment altogether, and when it comes to the latter, technical failures (such as mis-calibrations of instrumentation or other careless oversights) from personal failure. For scientists who are just starting to conduct real research – that is, research in which one does not know what to expect as an outcome, rather than the carefully controlled "experiments" students conduct in the lab solely as a way to learn good lab techniques – a series of setbacks or the failure of a major project can quickly lead to a lack of faith in the experimental process itself. Such failure can create a sense of anxiety over the future of the project, especially in an environment in which the need for funding creates a pressing need to generate positive results quickly. This mental and financial pressure robs the young scientist of the fundamental right of all experimenters: the right to make mistakes. The greatest scientific discoveries have come not after a carefully and elegantly controlled series of pre-planned steps, but rather through the lumpy, uneven process of trial-and-error in which serendipity plays a significant role. But to that scientist who learns the wrong lesson from failure too strongly and too early in their career, the basic enterprise of science ceases to be a learning from failure and instead simply becomes failure.

The scientists' main recourse is to simply recast all lab work as a learning process in which it is the process of experimenting itself that is a success, such that there are no failures. The real sense of oneself as a scientist comes from an ability to understand "failures" as a chance to learn either something about the mechanics of lab work, or something about the system being investigated. The exploration itself becomes the central process of developing the young scientist. If the scientist makes a technical mistake in the operation of a piece of lab equipment, it is an opportunity to develop the toolset that will allow future investigations to proceed more smoothly, whereas if the results are simply wildly different than expected, it gives the scientist an opportunity to investigate something new and interesting about the world. In either case, the central mental faculty being prodded is the scientist's primary tool: curiosity.

An openness and curiosity about the world itself is, of course, the primary motivator for most of those who embark on the scientific journey to begin with. And failure is not always a frustrating setback that many first believe. It was, after all, the failure of Alexander Fleming to properly care for his petri dishes that lead to the discovery of penicillin, or Wilson Greatbach's inadvertent use of a resistor a thousand times too strong that lead to the development of the pacemaker. These sparks of genius and the exhilaration they bring are scattered liberally throughout the entire history of science. Ironically, one of the great curses that can befall a fledgling scientist is to experience not a great stroke of failure at the start of his career, but rather one of these great strokes of luck. If the talented young researcher has such a lucky moment, and comes to believe that such breakthroughs are the normal course of affairs, he may come to think after a subsequent few years of failure that he critically lacks some skill at research and may be driven into a more reliable profession, such as science teaching or science journalism.

Anyone who has devoted their life's work to the laboratory must ultimately have a moment in their career when their curiosity about the research itself, rather than the accolades it may bring, creates a sense of joy. This joy for working in the lab, in which the enterprise ceases to be work and becomes neither a vocation nor an avocation and instead becomes simply a way of life, is the foundational basis for that critical transformation: from a mere technician to a true scientist. Whatever technical mishaps may happen, whatever moments of serendipity may arrive, and whatever the results may show or fail to show, it is the curiosity and joy of discovery that define the scientist.

[Adapted from *Failure Across Professions* Audrey O'Connell, Sussex County Historical Press, 1993]

1. In paragraph three, the author mentions a "failure" of Alexander Fleming and an "inadvertent" action by Wilson Greatbach. In context, these words suggest that at least part of scientific discovery:

A) requires making technical mistakes.

B) can only happen to fledgling scientists who have a great stroke of luck.

C) involves doing things that might typically be considered mistakes.

D) is motivated by a desire for accolades.

2. The author implies that scientists who persist in their careers as research scientists do so because they:

A) seek the accolades that come from making a major breakthrough.

B) are compelled by a sense of curiosity about the world.

C) would not be happy in a reliable profession such as teaching or journalism.

D) experience pressure to obtain funding by demonstrating positive results.

3. All of the following are stated in the passage EXCEPT:

A) Making discoveries in the lab creates a sense of curiosity about the world.

B) Failure to produce positive results quickly can discourage new scientists.

C) Recasting both technical failures and unexpected results as successes can encourage scientists.

D) Failure is not always a setback.

4. In another work, the author of the passage states that approximately half of promising young Ph.D. candidates who appear as second or third authors on research papers early in their studies eventually either fail to complete their degree or do so

without publishing any other original research. This is most likely due to:

A) new researchers failing to cultivate a sense of curiosity that lets failure be reinterpreted as success.

B) a stroke of serendipity occurring early in the career of young scientists.

C) a failure to distinguish between mere technical failures and a failure to achieve the expected results.

D) a desire to become either a science journalist or a science teacher.

5. One science journalist remarked, "no one likes the blind fumbling about that leads to the lucky discovery; everyone likes having made the lucky discovery". The passage suggests that fledgling scientists who prefer "having made the lucky discovery" might be expected:

A) to make more lucky discoveries.

B) to give up research science.

C) to increase their technical facility in the lab.

D) to develop a stronger curiosity about the world.

6. The passage most strongly supports which of the following in regards to scientists?

A) They frequently experience failure through the process of trial-and-error.

B) Some of the greatest scientists had sloppy lab technique that lead to technical failure.

C) Whether or not one achieves great success as a scientist depends solely on luck.

D) Their work transforms who they are by transforming their way of life.

7. Which of the following, if true, would most *weaken* the assertions made by the author?

A) Scientists should treat the lab as something of a playground in which their imagination can be given free rein.

B) A scientist prone to technical errors is displaying a personal failure through carelessness and should seek another line of work.

C) Scientists must cultivate a deep sense of patience since the lucky discovery may come along only after many years.

D) A scientist is fundamentally an explorer and is at her best when she is off the map: there can be no mistakes because there are no lines to cross.

Highlighting Practice Passage II

Bright young scientists must learn through trial-and-error to separate failure to achieve the expected results from failure of the experiment altogether, and when it comes to the latter, technical failures (such as mis-calibrations of instrumentation or other careless oversights) from personal failure. For scientists who are just starting to conduct real research – that is, research in which one does not know what to expect as an outcome, rather than the carefully controlled "experiments" students conduct in the lab solely as a way to learn good lab techniques – a series of setbacks or the failure of a major project can quickly lead to a lack of faith in the experimental process itself. Such failure can create a sense of anxiety over the future of the project, especially in an environment in which the need for funding creates a pressing need to generate positive results quickly. This mental and financial pressure robs the young scientist of the fundamental right of all experimenters: the right to make mistakes. The greatest scientific discoveries have come not after a carefully and elegantly controlled series of pre-planned steps, but rather through the lumpy, uneven process of trial-and-error in which serendipity plays a significant role. But to that scientist who learns the wrong lesson from failure too strongly and too early in their career, the basic enterprise of science ceases to be a learning from failure and instead simply becomes failure.

Scratch Notes: Failing can cause scientists to feel pressured and to give up. Real discov. from trial-and-error + luck.

The scientists' main recourse is to simply recast all lab work as a learning process in which it is the process of experimenting itself that is a success, such that there are no failures. The real sense of oneself as a scientist comes from an ability to understand "failures" as a chance to learn either something about the mechanics of lab work, or something about the system being investigated. The exploration itself becomes the central process of developing the young scientist. If the scientist makes a technical mistake in the operation of a piece of lab equipment, it is an opportunity to develop the toolset that will allow future investigations to proceed more smoothly, whereas if the results are simply wildly different than expected, it gives the scientist an opportunity to investigate something new and interesting about the world. In either case, the central mental faculty being prodded is the scientist's primary tool: curiosity.

Scratch Notes: Auth thinks new sci. need dev. curiosity + see fail as chance to learn.

An openness and curiosity about the world itself is, of course, the primary motivator for most of those who embark on the scientific journey to begin with. And failure is not always a frustrating setback that many first believe. It was, after all, the failure of Alexander **Fleming** to properly care for his petri dishes that lead to the discovery of penicillin, or Wilson **Greatbach's** inadvertent use of a resistor a thousand times too strong that lead to the development of the pacemaker. These sparks of genius and the exhilaration they bring are scattered liberally throughout the entire history of science. Ironically, one of the great curses that can befall a fledgling scientist is to experience not a great stroke of failure at the start of his career, but rather one of these great strokes of luck. If the talented young researcher has such a lucky moment, and comes to believe that such breakthroughs are the normal course of affairs, he may come to think after a subsequent few years of failure that he critically lacks some skill at research and may be driven into a more reliable profession, such as science teaching or science journalism.

Scratch Notes: Great luck at start of career can be bad. Journalism + teaching more reliable jobs. Curiosity in the first place drives ppl to sci.

Anyone who has devoted their life's work to the laboratory must ultimately have a moment in their career when their curiosity about the research itself, rather than the accolades it may bring, creates a sense of joy. This joy for working in the lab, in which the enterprise ceases to be work and becomes neither a vocation nor an avocation and instead becomes simply a way of life, is the foundational basis for that critical transformation: from a mere technician to a true scientist. Whatever technical mishaps may happen, whatever moments of serendipity may arrive, and whatever the results may show or fail to show, it is the curiosity and joy of discovery that define the scientist.

[Adapted from *Failure Across Professions* Audrey O'Connell, Sussex County Historical Press, 1993]

Scratch Notes: Auth. - curiosity and lab research as a way of life def. of true scientist.

Main Idea: The process of becoming a true scientist is one in which native curiosity is channeled into lab work and failures are seen as a chance to learn more.

1. In paragraph three, the author mentions a "failure" of Alexander Fleming and an "inadvertent" action by Wilson Greatbach. In context, these words suggest that at least part of scientific discovery:

A) requires making technical mistakes.

B) can only happen to fledgling scientists who have a great stroke of luck.

C) involves doing things that might typically be considered mistakes.

D) is motivated by a desire for accolades.

The author begins paragraph three by telling us that failure is a part of the scientific process of discovery, and gives us Fleming and Greatbach as examples of that "failure". Choice C matches.

A: This choice is close but we don't know that Fleming and Greatbach made "technical" mistakes. The more open language of "might" in choice C is better.

B: "Only" is too strong. We also don't know that Fleming or Greatbach was a fledgling scientist at the time.

D: We're not told that Fleming or Greatbach sought accolades.

2. The author implies that scientists who persist in their careers as research scientists do so because they:

A) seek the accolades that come from making a major breakthrough.

B) are compelled by a sense of curiosity about the world.

C) would not be happy in a reliable profession such as teaching or journalism.

D) experience pressure to obtain funding by demonstrating positive results.

The overall main theme repeated throughout the passage is one of curiosity driving people into science and then motivating them as scientists. That's choice B.

3. All of the following are stated in the passage EXCEPT:

A) Making discoveries in the lab creates a sense of curiosity about the world.

B) Failure to produce positive results quickly can discourage new scientists.

C) Recasting both technical failures and unexpected results as successes can encourage scientists.

D) Failure is not always a setback.

Choice A is the opposite of the author's contention. He mentions that being curious is what pushes people into the scientific enterprise in the first place but choice A gets that backwards.

B: Mentioned in the first paragraph.

C, D: Mentioned throughout.

4. In another work, the author of the passage states that approximately half of promising young Ph.D. candidates who appear as second or third authors on research papers early in their studies eventually either fail to complete their degree or do so without publishing any other original research. This is most likely due to:

A) new researchers failing to cultivate a sense of curiosity that lets failure be reinterpreted as success.

B) a stroke of serendipity occurring early in the career of young scientists.

C) a failure to distinguish between mere technical failures and a failure to achieve the expected results.

D) a desire to become either a science journalist or a science teacher.

The author's overall theme is that cultivating a curiosity about the world and finding meaning in the lab work itself is what scientists find as the reward, and that this faith in the process itself helps them reinterpret failure as success. If a promising candidate eventually gives up, it most likely indicates choice A: that they haven't been able to develop that ability to recast failure as success.

5. One science journalist remarked, "no one likes the blind fumbling about that leads to the lucky discovery; everyone likes having made the lucky discovery". The passage suggests that fledgling scientists who prefer "having made the lucky discovery" might be expected:

A) to make more lucky discoveries.

B) to give up research science.

C) to increase their technical facility in the lab.

D) to develop a stronger curiosity about the world.

The author's main theme throughout is that true scientists come to care more about the process of lab work itself, rather than any accolades that develop. So a young scientist who fails to generate this appreciation for the process itself is unlikely to stick with it. Thus choice B is correct.

6. The passage most strongly supports which of the following in regards to scientists?

   A) They frequently experience failure through the process of trial-and-error.

   B) Some of the greatest scientists had sloppy lab technique that lead to technical failure.

   C) Whether or not one achieves great success as a scientist depends solely on luck.

   D) Their work transforms who they are by transforming their way of life.

The passage tells us right in the first paragraph that science often proceeds through a lumpy uneven process of trial and error. The author mentions this in the context of telling us how often science can generate failure in the lab. This is presented as the normal course of affairs, not something unusual. Thus choice A is true.

   B: We're given examples of some sloppy technique, but those sloppy techniques lead to huge breakthroughs, not to failure.

   C: "Solely" is too extreme here.

   D: This is both too strong and gets the causality backwards. The author tells us that being curious in the first place drives someone to being a scientist, not that being a scientist makes them curious.

7. Which of the following, if true, would most *weaken* the assertions made by the author?

A) Scientists should treat the lab as something of a playground in which their imagination can be given free rein.

B) A scientist prone to technical errors is displaying a personal failure through carelessness and should seek another line of work.

C) Scientists must cultivate a deep sense of patience since the lucky discovery may come along only after many years.

D) A scientist is fundamentally an explorer and is at her best when she is off the map: there can be no mistakes because there are no lines to cross.

This question asks us to weaken the author's point of view. Choice B is just about the exact opposite of the author's main idea and thus if it were true it would sink the whole passage. Thus choice B is correct.

A, D: These align perfectly with the author's main idea.

C: The author doesn't directly address patience, but he does emphasize the importance of lucky discoveries. It follows, then, that sticking to it waiting for the lucky discovery is a good trait for scientists.

Approach III: The Skimming Technique

Some students cannot let themselves answer a question without obsessively checking and re-checking the passage. In my decades of MCAT experience, I've learned it's easier to accommodate that particular OCD demon than it is to exorcise it.

Passage: 2 minutes

Highlighter: Just key terms – proper nouns, etc.

Booklet: don't use

Question: 8 minutes

With the skimming approach, your goal is to zip through the passage, only reading the first couple of lines of each paragraph and the last couple of lines of each paragraph. The idea is to just get a very, very loose general sense of what's going on.

Then get to the questions ASAP. You'll want to read the questions slowly and carefully. Give yourself plenty of time go back and look stuff up. By the time you're done with the question set you'll probably end up reading or re-reading most of the passage.

For the following practice passages, we've slightly greyed-out portions of the passage. We're showing you where you should skim over when you're first reading through the passage. That is, your skim should be focused on the beginnings and ends of paragraphs, and skip over the greyed-out middle of the paragraphs.

In the explanations that follow, we include the full notations of **bold, underlined** terms in the text that we use to indicate highlighting and **bold, italic** text after each paragraph. These notations are not meant to suggest you should have done any highlighting or note-taking while skimming. Instead, these are key ideas that you should have found when going back to the passage to answer the questions.

Skimming Practice Passage I

In his recent book, *The Genius of Dogs: How Dogs are Smarter than You Think*, Brian Hare argues that the communicative abilities of dogs extend well past the blunt signifiers of tail and ear position and bared teeth that humans have long known. If you ask the typical lay person, they would suggest that dog vocalizations consist of little more than barking, growling, and whining. And while Hare's work doesn't expand on this basic repertoire, he convincingly argues that dogs are communicating far more than we were previously aware, through some combination of pitch, loudness and timbre.

Even many dog owners think that a dog's bark contains very little information. That is, the dog isn't "thinking" anything in particular, nor trying to communicate anything in particular. They bark just because "that's what dogs do". Research by Raymond Coppinger seems to support what he calls an "arousal model". That is, dogs simply bark when they're excited about something, and the barking is not a behavior over which the dog is exerting any conscious control and with no attempt at communication by the dog. In support of his hypothesis, Coppinger presents data gathered from several different breeds of working dogs whose job is to protect free-range livestock. In many instances, the dogs barked nearly continuously for six to eight hours, even when no other dogs or humans were within earshot. The bark simply communicates the fact that the barking dog is excited, with no attempt to communicate that message to any particular audience. Hare provides an anecdote which seems to align with the arousal model: he talks about a guard dog he had while working in Africa who would bark at every passerby throughout the night, even when they were people the dog had known and lived with for years.

More recent research, however, suggests that barking and growling may communicate more than had been previously thought. Dogs' vocal cords are highly flexible, permitting dogs to alter their vocalizations to produce a wide variety of different sounds. Scientists recorded the barking and growling done by dogs under a variety of situations. One involved a recording of a "food growl" and a "stranger growl". The first was recorded when researchers attempted to take food away from an aggressive dog, and the second when they simply approached aggressive dogs. They then placed food on the opposite side of the room from another dog and let it approach the food. They played back recordings of both the "stranger" and "food" growls as the dogs approached the food. Only in response to the "food" growl did the dogs hesitate before continuing.

In a similar experiment, researchers recorded the barks of dogs in two different situations. In the first, the dogs were simply left alone. In the second, a stranger would approach the dog, eliciting barking. When those barks were played later for other dogs, these other dogs ignored all of the "alone" barking, but perked up immediately when the "stranger" bark was played. Even more surprising, humans were able to distinguish between the barks, and correctly identify which was which, even if the human test subjects were not themselves dog owners.

Hare also notes that barking behavior itself seems to be an unintended consequence of domestication. While wolves and dogs share many behavioral characteristics (and, in fact, dogs were reclassified in 1993 as a subspecies of wolf), wolves rarely bark. Barking makes up only a small percent – by Hare's estimates as low as 3% – of wolf vocalizations. In addition, the experimental foxes in Russia that have been "force domesticated" over the span of just a handful of generations have shown the same split: the wild-type foxes don't bark, whereas the domesticated ones do. The artificial selection process that selects against aggression and fear in canids seems to have unearthed a propensity for barking.

[Adapted from "Sparky Speaks?" by Elliot Hirsen, 2011]

1. Based on the information in the passage, the presence of barking behavior in the absence of other dogs or humans supports the idea that:

   A) dogs' highly flexible vocal cords permit them to bark for a variety of purposes.

   B) some barking behavior indicates the emotional state of the dog without communicative intent.

   C) the arousal model fails to account for a common observation made by dog owners.

   D) Hare's work is fundamentally flawed.

2. The passage suggests that recordings of dogs barking, to be useful in studying dog communication, must be:

   A) made when attempting to take food away from a dog.

   B) of particularly high quality so as to be recognizable by other dogs.

   C) intelligible to a human audience.

   D) recorded in response to a specific situation being studied.

3. Animal researchers have recorded a set of vocalizations made by hyenas in conjunction with several different hyena behaviors commonly exhibited in the wild. If the researchers wanted to speculate on the function of those vocalizations, Hare would suggest that they:

A) play those recordings to human listeners and ask the humans to distinguish between the vocalizations.

B) use a spectrograph to analyze the pitch, loudness, or timbre of the vocalizations.

C) compare the vocalization behavior of hyenas with their nearest domesticated relative.

D) play those recordings to other hyenas and observe their reactions.

4. Based on the passage, which of the following pieces of background knowledge would be most helpful in evaluating Hare's contentions?

A) Knowledge of how vocalization developed as a communication tool in people

B) An understanding of the different sorts of jobs for which dogs have been bred

C) A familiarity with the normal set of behaviors and vocalizations exhibited by wolves

D) A familiarity with the skeletal anatomy of a typical dog

5. Which of the following would most strengthen Coppinger's theory about the function of barking?

A) There are perceptible differences in the barks of dogs who are being threatened by larger animals and those being threatened by smaller animals.

B) When fed a slight sedative, the barking activity of dogs tended to increase in response to strangers.

C) Wolves show an increased amount of barking when kept in captivity.

D) When given food that contained small doses of stimulant drugs but provided with no environmental cues, dogs increased the duration and frequency of their barking.

Skimming Practice Passage I

In his recent book, **The Genius of Dogs: How Dogs are Smarter than You Think**, **Brian Hare** argues that the **communicative abilities of dogs extend** well past the blunt signifiers of tail and ear position and bared teeth that humans have long known. If you ask the typical lay person, they would suggest that dog vocalizations consist of little more than barking, growling, and whining. And while Hare's work **doesn't expand on this basic repertoire**, he convincingly argues that **dogs are communicating far more** than we were previously aware, through some combination of pitch, loudness and timbre.

Key terms: book title, Brian Hare

Opinion: Hare thinks dogs communicate a lot with their vocalizations

Even many dog owners think that a **dog's bark contains very little information**. That is, the dog isn't "thinking" anything in particular, nor trying to communicate anything in particular. They bark just because "that's what dogs do". Research by **Raymond Coppinger** seems to support what he calls an "**arousal model**". That is, dogs simply **bark when they're excited** about something, and the barking is not a behavior over which the dog is exerting any conscious control and with **no attempt at communication by the dog**. In support of his hypothesis, Coppinger presents data gathered from several different breeds of working dogs whose job is to protect **free-range livestock**. In many instances, the dogs barked nearly continuously for six to eight hours, even when no other dogs or humans were within earshot. The bark simply communicates the fact that **the barking dog is excited**, with no attempt to communicate that message to any particular audience. Hare provides an anecdote which seems to align with the arousal model: he talks about a guard dog he had while working in Africa who would bark at every passerby throughout the night, even when they were people the dog had known and lived with for years.

Key terms: Coppinger, arousal model, livestock

Opinion: Coppinger thinks barking just means dog is excited with no communication behind it

More recent research, however, suggests that **barking and growling may communicate more** than had been previously thought. Dogs' **vocal cords** are highly flexible, permitting dogs to alter their vocalizations to produce a wide variety of different sounds. Scientists recorded the barking and growling done by dogs under a variety of situations. One involved a recording of a **"food growl" and a "stranger growl"**. The first was recorded when researchers attempted to take food away from an aggressive dog, and the second when they simply approached aggressive dogs. They then placed food on the opposite side of the room from another dog and let it approach the food. They played back recordings of both the "stranger" and "food" growls as the dogs approached the food. **Only in response to the "food" growl did the dogs hesitate** before continuing.

Key terms: vocal cords, food growl, stranger growl

Cause-and-effect: recording of food growl made other dogs hesitate before approaching food, stranger growl didn't

In a similar experiment, researchers recorded the barks of dogs in two different situations. In the first, the dogs were simply left alone. In the second, a stranger would approach the dog, eliciting barking. When those barks were played later for other **dogs, these other dogs ignored all of the "alone" barking**, but perked up immediately when the "stranger" bark was played. Even more surprising, **humans were able to distinguish** between the barks, and correctly identify which was which, even if the human test subjects were not themselves dog owners.

Cause-and-effect: along barking got no response from other dogs, but stranger barking did, humans were able to distinguish

Hare also notes that barking behavior itself seems to be an **unintended consequence of domestication**. While wolves and dogs share many behavioral characteristics (and, in fact, dogs were reclassified in 1993 as a **subspecies of wolf**), **wolves rarely bark**. Barking makes up only a small percent – by Hare's estimates as low as 3% – of wolf vocalizations. In addition, the experimental foxes in Russia that have been "force domesticated" over the span of just a handful of generations have shown the same split: the **wild-type foxes don't bark, whereas the domesticated ones do**. The artificial selection process that selects against aggression and fear in canids seems to have unearthed a propensity for barking.

[Adapted from "Sparky Speaks?" by Elliot Hirsen, 2011]

Cause-and-effect: domestication creates barking behavior

Contrast: wolves and wild foxes don't bark, dogs and domesticated foxes do

Main Idea: Dog vocalizations communicate more than we previously thought, and although dogs sometimes bark in response to general excitement, they are capable of barking to communicate a variety of different situations.

1. Based on the information in the passage, the presence of barking behavior in the absence of other dogs or humans supports the idea that:

A) dogs' highly flexible vocal cords permit them to bark for a variety of purposes.

B) some barking behavior indicates the emotional state of the dog without communicative intent.

C) the arousal model fails to account for a common observation made by dog owners.

D) Hare's work is fundamentally flawed.

The question makes specific reference to an example of dog barking from Coppinger's studies. As Coppinger stated, dogs bark in response to general arousal (emotional state) without communicating anything in particular, as choice B says.

2. The passage suggests that recordings of dogs barking, to be useful in studying dog communication, must be:

A) made when attempting to take food away from a dog.

B) of particularly high quality so as to be recognizable by other dogs.

C) intelligible to a human audience.

D) **recorded in response to a specific situation being studied.**

In analyzing the various types of barking, the researches played the recordings of the barking back for other dogs to hear and for other humans. So both choice B and C seem tempting, but we can eliminate them both. After all, if C were correct, then B would also have to be correct. You can't have two right answers! Instead, we have to think not about who the recordings were played for, but when and why they were recorded – in response to different situations. Choice D nails it.

3. Animal researchers have recorded a set of vocalizations made by hyenas in conjunction with several different hyena behaviors commonly exhibited in the wild. If the researchers wanted to speculate on the function of those vocalizations, Hare would suggest that they:

A) play those recordings to human listeners and ask the humans to distinguish between the vocalizations.

B) use a spectrograph to analyze the pitch, loudness, or timbre of the vocalizations.

C) compare the vocalization behavior of hyenas with their nearest domesticated relative.

D) **play those recordings to other hyenas and observe their reactions.**

We must apply the technique used in the passage to a new situation. In the passage, the study was done by recording a dog's barks and then playing those barks back to listeners – first other dogs, then people who interact with dogs. A similar protocol would be choice D, to play hyena vocalizations back for other hyenas.

4. Based on the passage, which of the following pieces of background knowledge would be most helpful in evaluating Hare's contentions?

   A) Knowledge of how vocalization developed as communication tool in people

   B) An understanding of the different sorts of jobs for which dogs have been bred

   C) A familiarity with the normal set of behaviors and vocalizations exhibited by wolves

   D) A familiarity with the skeletal anatomy of a typical dog

The passage tells us that dogs are a subset of wolves, and Hare contends that barking serves as a communication tool, with different types of barks associated with different types of behaviors or situations. A relevant set of background data would be how wolves vocalize in response to different situations.

A, B, D: These are all only very tangentially related to dog vocalization.

5. Which of the following would most strengthen Coppinger's theory about the function of barking?

   A) There are perceptible differences in the barks of dogs who are being threatened by larger animals and those being threatened by smaller animals.

   B) When fed a slight sedative, the barking activity of dogs tended to increase in response to strangers.

   C) Wolves show an increased amount of barking when kept in captivity.

D) When given food that contained small doses of stimulant drugs but provided with no environmental cues, dogs increased the duration and frequency of their barking.

Coppinger's theory was that barking simply indicates arousal. Thus he would suggest that feeding dogs a stimulant would lead to more barking behavior, even in the absence of any particular signals from people or other dogs. Choice D nails it.

A: This suggests communication by the dog, which is the opposite of Coppinger's theory.

B: This is the opposite of what Coppinger would suggest. A sedative would reduce arousal.

Skimming Practice Passage II

As one looks forward to the America of fifty years hence, the main source of anxiety appears to be in a probable excess of prosperity, and in the want of a good grievance. We seem nearly at the end of those great public wrongs which require a special moral earthquake to end them. There seems nothing left which need be absolutely fought for; no great influence to keep us from a commonplace and perhaps debasing success. There will, no doubt, be still need of the statesman to adjust the details of government, and of the clergyman to keep an eye on private morals, including his own. There will also be social and religious changes, perhaps great ones; but there are no omens of any very fierce upheaval. And seeing the educational value to this generation of the reforms for which it has contended, one must feel an impulse of pity for our successors, who seem likely to have no convictions that they can honestly be mobbed for.

Can we spare these great tonics? It is the experience of history that all religious bodies are purified by persecution, and materialized by peace. No amount of accumulated virtue has thus far saved the merely devout communities from deteriorating, when let alone, into comfort and good dinners. This is most noticeable in detached organizations,—Moravians, Shakers, Quakers, Roman Catholics,—

they all go the same way at last; when persecution and missionary toil are over, they enter on a tiresome millennium of meat and pudding. To guard against this spiritual obesity, this carnal Eden, what has the next age in reserve for us? Suppose however many million perfectly healthy and virtuous Americans, what is to keep them from being as uninteresting as so many Chinese?

I know of nothing but that aim which is the climax and flower of all civilization, without which purity itself grows dull and devotion tedious,—the pursuit of Science and Art. Give to all this nation peace, freedom, prosperity, and even virtue, still there must be some absorbing interest, some career. That career can be sought only in two directions,—more and yet more material prosperity on the one side. Science and Art on the other. Every man's aim must either be riches, or something better than riches. To advocate the alternative career, the striving of the whole nature after something utterly apart from this world's wealth,—it is for this end that a stray voice is needed. It will not take long; the clamor of the market will re-absorb us to-morrow.

[Adapted from "Literature as an Art", *The Atlantic Monthly*, December, 1867.]

1. The author's primary purpose in this passage is:
  A) to provide a call to arms for individuals to follow passionate, challenging lives.
  B) to draw attention to the dramatic irony of a society starved for evil.
  C) to acknowledge the death of art as the bittersweet but necessary price of peace and justice.
  D) to argue for Science and Art as the inevitable flower and final purpose of a mature civilization.

2. Which of the following, if true, would most weaken the passage author's main argument?

A) Moravians, Quakers, and Roman Catholics are found to have most increased their prosperity in peacetime.

B) During the last US-involved war, sculpture increased while live theater decreased.

C) Hemingway's greatest novel, A Farewell to Arms, was based on his experiences in the Great War.

D) A national survey shows that individuals insulated from social upheaval are rated as the most passionate.

3. Which of the following assumptions does the author make in the first paragraph?

A) Challenging but laudable tasks benefit those who undertake them.

B) Later generations are as likely to have strong moral convictions as the current one.

C) A strong moral imperative can be gained from experience.

D) Moral conviction is less desirable than an easy life.

4. According to the passage, which of the following exemplifies the decline of a people or organization after its battles are won and trials endured?

A) The safe, boring lives of millions of Chinese.

B) The debasing success of America's latest moral earthquake.

C) The Shaker's post-missionary-phase millennium of prosperity.

D) The increase of peacetime science.

5. Which of the following does the passage author assume to be true, based on the second paragraph?

A) China has never experienced war or serious social upheaval.

B) Hard-earned virtue is preferable to meaningless ease.

C) The Quakers have become materialistic and complacent.

D) Pudding is contradictory to revolution.

6. In context, when the passage describes a "spiritual obesity, a carnal Eden", the author means

A) that without some bitterness in life, the sweet can never be as sweet.

B) that an excess of prosperity can lead to spiritual ill-health.

C) that paradise on Earth is a part of humanity's future, rather than its past.

D) that austerity, not prosperity, is necessary for moral uprightness.

7. Suppose a survey of Spanish poetry from the 13th to 21st century revealed the frequency of highly-acclaimed and widely reprinted work (relative to the amount published during the period) spiked during revolutionary periods. The passage author would likely explain this as:

A) the result of unjust circumstances fostering a passion for truth and moral right.

B) a result of the lack of lucrative employment making the arts more desirable.

C) an anomaly, explainable by the heterogeneity of a nation in crisis.

D) a result of a greater demand for beautiful things in difficult times.

Skimming Practice Passage II

As one looks forward to the **America of fifty years hence**, the main source of anxiety appears to be in a probable **excess of prosperity**, and in the **want of a good grievance**. We seem nearly at the end of those great **public wrongs** which require a special **moral earthquake** to end them. There seems nothing left which need be absolutely fought for; no great influence to keep us from a commonplace and perhaps **debasing success**. There will, no doubt, be still need of the statesman to adjust the details of government, and of the clergyman to keep an eye on private morals, including his own. There will also be social and religious changes, perhaps great ones; but there are no omens of any very fierce upheaval. And seeing the **educational value** to this generation of the **reforms** for which it has contended, one must feel an impulse of pity for our successors, who seem likely to have no **convictions** that they can honestly be mobbed for.

Key terms: America, public wrongs, moral earthquake, reforms, convictions

Contrast: contradictory terms: excess of good, want of bad, debasing success;

Cause-and-effect: peace and prosperity give future generations no chance for education/conviction

Opinion: individual greatness requires difficult times

Can we spare these great tonics? It is the experience of history that all religious bodies are **purified by persecution**, and **materialized by peace**. No amount of accumulated virtue has thus far saved the merely devout communities from **deteriorating**, when let alone, into comfort and good dinners. This is most noticeable in detached organizations,—**Moravians, Shakers, Quakers, Roman Catholics**,—they all go the same way at last; when persecution and missionary toil are over, they enter on a **tiresome** millennium of meat and pudding. To guard against this **spiritual obesity**, this **carnal Eden**, what has the next age in reserve for us? Suppose however many million perfectly healthy and virtuous **Americans**, what is to keep them from being as uninteresting as so many **Chinese**?

Key terms: purified, Moravians, Shakers, Quakers, Roman Catholics, Eden, Chinese

Contrast: persecution purifies but peace leads to materialism; virtuous and persecuted Americans, boring (stable, wealthy?) Chinese

Cause-and-effect: when no trials are left, groups and individuals become complacent and weak; spoils of victory destroy virtuous qualities

Opinion: turbulence and difficulty creates the best individuals; wealthy and peaceful are to be pitied for weakness

I know of nothing but that aim which is the climax and **flower of all civilization**, without which purity itself grows dull and devotion tedious,—the pursuit of **Science and Art**. Give to all this nation peace, freedom, prosperity, and even virtue, still there must be some absorbing interest, some career. That career can be sought only in two directions,—more and yet more **material prosperity** on the one side. Science and Art on the other. Every man's aim must either be riches, or something better than riches. To advocate the alternative career, the striving of the whole nature after something utterly apart from this world's wealth,—it is for this end that **a stray voice is needed**. It will not take long; the clamor of the market will re-absorb us to-morrow.

Key terms: civilization, Science, Art

Contrast: riches vs. something better

Cause-and-effect: lack of great war or social cause implies need for worthwhile individual pursuits

Opinion: art and science are the greatest pursuits; material prosperity is tempting but art is better

Main Idea: a society with no injustice, no pain, no evil, is at risk of losing its greatness, so one must advocate the pursuit of greatness through art and science

1. The author's primary purpose in this passage is:

   A) to provide a call to arms for individuals to follow passionate, challenging lives.

   B) to draw attention to the dramatic irony of a society starved for evil.

   C) to acknowledge the death of art as the bittersweet but necessary price of peace and justice.

   D) to argue for Science and Art as the inevitable flower and final purpose of a mature civilization.

At first glance, A , B, and C all seem relatively close matches for the main idea of the passage. D is almost exactly lifted from the passage, and is found in the concluding paragraph, however it doesn't fully encapsulate the main idea. However, it does show why A is the best match. The passage author not only elucidates the problem of a society with no more physical or moral battles to fight, he advocates a solution, which A is a reasonably good match for. He does not discuss the problem merely to make a point of its irony (B), nor to reluctantly accept it as an inevitability (C).

2. Which of the following, if true, would most weaken the passage author's main argument?

A) Moravians, Quakers, and Roman Catholics are found to have most increased their prosperity in peacetime.

B) During the last US-involved war, sculpture increased while live theater decreased.

C) Hemingway's greatest novel, A Farewell to Arms, was based on his experiences in the Great War.

D) A national survey shows that individuals insulated from social upheaval are rated as the most passionate.

The main argument is that great societal challenges such as war or social injustices that need changing provide a sort of moral education for the citizens who experience and face these great tasks, and, as a corollary, that the lack of such crises denies individuals the opportunity to learn virtue and conviction. Either evidence of a society with great challenges but little moral conviction, or a society without such challenges whose citizens nevertheless have great moral conviction, would weaken the argument. D is a pretty good match for the latter and, if true, would weaken the main argument. Both A and B are neutral, neither strengthening nor weakening the main argument, while C actually strengthens it.

3. Which of the following assumptions does the author make in the first paragraph?

A) Challenging but laudable tasks benefit those who undertake them.

B) Later generations are as likely to have strong moral convictions as the current one.

C) A strong moral imperative can be gained from experience.

D) Moral conviction is less desirable than an easy life.

A is not an assumption but an explicit statement. B is contrary to what the passage suggests in the first paragraph. But the first paragraph notes the educational value of the fight for reforms, stating that those who come later, in the peaceful era, will lack conviction. The implication is that the lack of such experiences will be responsible for the lack of conviction, which assumes that moral conviction can be learned, matching the statement in C. D is the exact opposite of another assumption the author makes, given the comment about pitying those who come later.

4. According to the passage, which of the following exemplifies the decline of a people or organization after its battles are won and trials endured?

A) The safe, boring lives of millions of Chinese.

B) The debasing success of America's latest moral earthquake.

C) The Shaker's post-missionary-phase millennium of prosperity.

D) The increase of peacetime science.

Since the question stem specifically asks about the decline of a people, the answer choice must reflect the time of stability after all the battles are won. There was no mention in the passage itself of what previous trials and tribulations the Chinese have or have not faced, so A can be eliminated. America's recent social upheaveal is mentioned, but the expected decline is hypothetical and lies still in the future, so B is not a good match either. C is a perfect match, and is found in the passage. D is offered in the passage as a cure for such a decline, not a sign of it.

5. Which of the following does the passage author assume to be true, based on the second paragraph?

  A) China has never experienced war or serious social upheaval.

  B) Hard-earned virtue is preferable to meaningless ease.

  C) The Quakers have become materialistic and complacent.

  D) Pudding is contradictory to revolution.

Since the answer choices come from different parts of the paragraph, it's necessary to examine them one at a time. A is very tempting, as the author compares citizens of a turbulent America to those of China, suggesting that the latter country has been stable and free of war (and its citizens consequently boring). However, this does not necessarily mean that the country has never faced war or upheaval, only that it has not in the most recent generation at the time the passage was written. B, however, is assumed, given the tone of the passage. In this paragraph, the passage author describes a life of peace and material ease as tiresome, deteriorated, and boring. The author is operating under the assumption that such a life is undesirable. C is a consequence of that same assumption, and is outright stated, not assumed. D might be tempting, but on closer examination it is not integral to the argument. Although pudding is used as an example or indicator of sloth and complacency, it's not the main point. The author is not arguing against eating pudding, but against a life where everything is easy and passion has no place. It's not necessary to assume that a revolutionary cannot have the occasional pudding.

6. In context, when the passage describes a "spiritual obesity, a carnal Eden", the author means

  A) that without some bitterness in life, the sweet can never be as sweet.

  B) that an excess of prosperity can lead to spiritual ill-health.

C) that paradise on Earth is a part of humanity's future, rather than its past.

D) that austerity, not prosperity, is necessary for moral uprightness.

The author's colorful phrasing, a "spiritual obesity", uses the metaphor of overindulgence causing ill health to describe the surprising results of achieving prosperity and peace. The purpose of the passage is to warn against this danger, and the purpose of the quoted phrase is to sum up the problem, which is well-stated in B. Answer choice A sounds reasonable based on the phrasing itself, but does not match any of the arguments in the passage. C, too, is nowhere in the passage. D is tempting, as it nearly hits the passage author's main idea, but the problem is not the lack of "lack", but the lack of an actual injustice or challenge. The focus on prosperity versus austerity misses the mark somewhat.

7. Suppose a survey of Spanish poetry from the 13th to 21st century revealed the frequency of highly-acclaimed and widely reprinted work (relative to the amount published during the period) spiked during revolutionary periods. The passage author would likely explain this as

A) the result of unjust circumstances fostering a passion for truth and moral right.

B) a result of the lack of lucrative employment making the arts more desirable.

C) an anomaly, explainable by the heterogeneity of a nation in crisis.

D) a result of a greater demand for beautiful things in difficult times.

The passage author's main argument describes social turbulence and injustice as moral teachers, and the lack of them as leading to a bland, convictionless populace. It follows that individuals of passion and moral strength are disproportionately created—taught—during turbulent times. It's assumed that this creates better and more meaningful art. A is a good match for this. B is nowhere in the passage. C contradicts the main idea, which predicts this outcome rather than calling it an anomaly. D too is not in the passage.